North Western

A. E. Jones

Ian Allan PUBLISHING

Contents

First published 2008
ISBN 978 0 7110 3227 9

Published by Ian Allan Publishing an imprint of Ian Allan Publishing Ltd, Hersham, Surrey KT12 4RG

Printed in England by Ian Allan Printing Ltd, Hersham, Surrey KT12 4RG

Code: 0807/B

Visit the Ian Allan Publishing website at www.ianallanpublishing.com

Previous page: Shortly after delivery in 1949 a stylish Leyland PD2/Weymann glints in the sunshine in Manchester's Piccadilly bus station, ahead of a soon-to-be-rebodied prewar Bristol K5G/ECW on the 36 to Northwich. This terminus was described more accurately on North Western buses as 'Parker Street', rather than the generally used 'Piccadilly'. *J. W. Hillmer*

Mersey Square parking ground was a honey-pot for bus photographers, but this fine study is included for its fascinating content. From right to left are all-Leyland PD2 No 239 of 1949, Bristol K5G/Strachans semi-utility No 4 of 1942, 1949 Weymann-bodied PD2 No 259 (on the 28), 1939 Bristol K5G/ECW No 894 (on the 76), similar No 895 on the 27x, L5G/ECW No 189 of 1947, K5G/Strachans austerity No 8 of 1942 and Brush-rebodied JO5G No 767 of 1936. *J. W. Hillmer*

Introduction

North Western Road Car had a very distinctive character: pragmatic and down-to-earth and providing great interest to its observers whilst avoiding the elitist aura of Ribble or Southdown. It engendered great loyalty from country-dwellers to whom it gave mobility — and amongst its staff — and proved a fertile training-ground for many aspiring managers who later rose to eminence. If you wanted to get into Manchester quickly, on a 27 or 28 from the city side of Stockport, it was commonly said "You'll have to lie down in the road to get it to stop", but outbound every potential passenger was gathered in; duty boards were peppered with injunctions such as 'Wait for car from Congleton due at Monks Heath at 2.33pm', and such country connections were faithfully observed. Other distinctive features were the large number of services worked jointly with other operators and, from the early 1930s, the relatively high proportion of express services.

Typically, senior management ranged from the autocratic through the coolly professional to the paternal, but it was always a tight ship! When, c1960, the 40-hour week was introduced for office staff, eliminating regular Saturday work, a memo issued by the General Manager curtly stated: 'Now that the Directors in their generosity have agreed to a 40-hour week … they emphasise that they require the same amount of work to be done in the reduced hours as have been done in the former hours'. No getting off lightly there, then! Discipline was strict, even into the 1950s, when staff turnover was becoming a problem. It had been even tighter in the prewar days of job scarcity, when, for a significant period, one Altrincham conductor had been forced to cycle to work at Macclesfield (a good 17 miles away, mostly along unlit 'A' roads) as a penalty for reporting late for duty on several occasions! Little wonder that he later became a Union rep — but, to his credit, a fair and reasonable one.

Under the Willebrew ticket system, used from the early 1930s to 1958, conductors had to pay in 'blind'; 'overs' went into the company's coffers, but 'shorts' were deducted from wages and, if occurring other than rarely, would result in severe disciplinary action. Drinking in uniform, even when off-duty, was understandably forbidden, and legend had it that, on one occasion when he was paying some incognito visits across the territory, Traffic Manager John Green entered a pub at Lower Peover in deepest Cheshire to find the crew of the infrequent 104 service imbibing alcohol during their lonely layover. He opened the dialogue saying: "My name's Green — what's yours?", to which the men naïvely replied in unison: "Mine's a pint, please!" To no-one's surprise, both were summarily dismissed.

Sometimes, however, the iron hand was applied in a velvet glove. One such case involved a Buxton driver who regularly took his lady-friend for free trips on late turns, news of which eventually filtered 'upstairs'. Came the day, and two mobile inspectors drove out to a remote location on the Ashbourne–Buxton route, one dropping off where he would be seen as the bus diverted into a village, the other driving off out of sight. As intended, the driver saw the waiting inspector and hastily issued the lady with a ticket, unfortunately only part-way to Buxton. On boarding as the bus regained the main road, the inspector noted that her ticket was the last issued and checked her destination, which she gave as Hindlow. He stayed on the bus that far, made sure she alighted, and after the bus disappeared he was picked up by the other inspector. The lady was left by the roadside with no means of getting home, her bus having been the last of the day. It stopped the malpractice, ostensibly by chance, thus avoiding any industrial-relations issues, a disciplinary hearing and an inevitable sacking, at a time when drivers were difficult to replace. On the other hand, a more understanding attitude did prevail given the right circumstances. Allowing fellow staff to travel free on local services whilst off-duty went by 'on the nod'; after all, the inspectors themselves benefited from this practice. The same applied to policemen going on or off duty, to save them having to walk to their beat, for crews never knew when they might need a policeman.

In another pragmatic approach, a blind eye was turned to unconventional crewing arrangements at Castleton, in the Peak

---

Handwritten:
t. = £1.10.0
1½ = £2.5.0

CONDUCTORS' WAGES TABLES
(Fractions ½d. omitted)
RATES OF PAY EFFECTIVE FROM 27-7-57

Hours	Rate after 12 months' service C1 3s. 10⁴/₁₁d.	Rate after 6 months' service C2 3s. 9⁹/₁₁d.	Commencing Rate C3 3s. 9³/₁₁d.	Hours
44	8 10 0	8 8 0	8 6 0	44
45	8 13 10	8 11 9	8 9 9	45
46	8 17 8	8 15 7	8 13 6	46
47	9 1 7	8 19 5	8 17 3	47
48	9 5 5	9 3 3	9 1 1	48
49	9 9 3	9 7 1	9 4 10	49
50	9 13 2	9 10 10	9 8 7	50
51	9 17 0	9 14 8	9 12 4	51
52	10 0 10	9 18 6	9 16 2	52
53	10 4 9	10 2 4	9 19 11	53

Note: Hours worked after 1.0 p.m. on Saturdays (except for Private Hire, Excursions & Tours) are paid an added flat rate of 11d. per hr. (Effective from 24/8/57)

NORTH WESTERN ROAD CAR COMPANY LIMITED

GUIDE TO CALCULATION OF WAGES FOR CONDUCTORS

Effective from 27/7/57

Based on Agreements between the Company and the Transport and General Workers' Union now in force and subject to any alteration therein.

SECTION A

Depots where 6 day week is worked.
Wages are calculated in Weekly periods.
Hours due are shown on strip enclosed in wages packet each week.

How To Calculate Extra Time Payable
(Not applicable to Private Hire, Excursions and Tours)

1—Rest Day worked on Weekday (at Company's request).
2—Rest Day worked on Sunday (at Company's request).
3—Rest Day worked on Agreed Bank Holiday (at Company's request).
4—Hours worked on a Sunday (not being a Rest Day) and Hours worked on Agreed Bank Holiday (not being a Rest Day).
For the above, see paragraphs (1), (2), (3) & (4) in Section B of this Guide.
5—Hours worked in excess of 44 for Week (excluding Rest Days and spread-over allowance).
Time and ½ first 2 hours; Time and ½ thereafter.
Example:—3 hours in excess of 44.
Divide 1st 2 hours by 4 = 30 mins.
Divide rest (½ hour) by 2 = 30 mins.
Total extra time payable is 1 hour.

Form 599 A

District, because these worked to mutual benefit and probably saved much lost mileage. For some time the crews at the small 'dormy shed' there were all related to the Driver-in-Charge (with the unfortunate name of Skidmore), and the rosters provided by Charles Street were honoured in so far as they did not conflict with family priorities. However, the collective sense of responsibility ensured that all services ran as timetabled, if not necessarily by the nominated crews. Ultimately, of course, this cosy arrangement would be curtailed by the introduction of one-man operation.

The company fully recognised the loyalty of long-service staff and good safe-driving records, regularly holding dining functions for those who qualified. At an event held in January 1950 Managing Director T. R. Williams said that he knew of only one other company that enjoyed the same degree of camaraderie, fellowship and loyalty. Notwithstanding the disruption of World War 2, almost 100 staff had by then completed more than 25 years' service, including one who had started with the infant 'British' operation 36 years earlier. A conductor who started at Oldham in 1924 retired there in 1968 as Depot Inspector, having been only the second holder of the post in 44 years. Others who served North Western to their utmost ability with total loyalty for most (if not all) of their working lives included John Williamson, the first Superintendent of the coach station in Manchester, who held the post until retiring in 1958. Devotion to duty even went beyond retirement, for an ex-Altrincham inspector allegedly phoned his successor whenever he noticed a 37 to or from Warrington passing his 'Jolly Thresher' pub near Lymm more than a few minutes off schedule — and that was an 11-mile route which had only a 3-minute layover at the Warrington end, as well as having to cross Latchford swing bridge over the Manchester Ship Canal, frequently closed for the passage of 10,000-ton ships!

Management and staff kept their ears well to the ground.

The 'Buxton driver' incident referred to in the text occurred in territory similar to that depicted in this scene near Earl Sterndale, featuring 1949 Bristol L5G/Weymann No 201 in its final months of service on a short-working of the Ashbourne–Buxton route in May 1963. *A. Moyes*

AEC Reliance 722 in latter-day livery spent time outstationed at Castleton and represented Weymann's final delivery of 20 saloons, with smoother front-end styling as supplied to fellow BET company Aldershot & District. *F. P. Roberts*

Depot inspectors had almost overwhelming responsibilities, working up to 75 hours and being always on call for scarcely £4 a week in the 1920s and early '30s. In many respects the bedrock of the company's operations, they were responsible for local 'hiring, firing and discipline', maintaining roadside stop signs and timetables, dealing with (or passing to HQ) public letters, complaints, items in local papers and details of competing rail and coach excursions; also ordering consumables, keeping alert to hearsay on local developments, assessing new traffic opportunities, keeping an eye on loadings (and arranging augmentation when necessary), carrying out revenue checks on the road and ensuring security of premises, vehicles, equipment, tickets and cash. Yet such men were intensely loyal, regarding all competitors as 'the enemy'. Their real reward was job satisfaction through having a high degree of local autonomy.

It was also notable that at any fund-raising local carnival — far more commonplace before NHS days — a company bus would

▲ Contrasting starkly with the rural idyll portrayed opposite, the vast bulk of the Metropolitan Vickers complex in grimy Trafford Park, Manchester, dwarfs Bristol K5G 422, supplied with an ECW body as No 894 in 1938. Still running in March 1963, by dint of a new Willowbrook body fitted 11 years earlier, it would be withdrawn that autumn. Service 68 was a peak-only link with Urmston and Flixton, operated jointly with Lancashire United and Manchester Corporation. *Author*

◄ Tilling-Stevens No 298 dated from 1928 but after rebodying in 1935 was chosen as the illuminated bus for the Silver Jubilee of King George V and Queen Mary in May of that year. Exactly two years later it would serve in a similar role to celebrate the Coronation of King George VI and Queen Elizabeth. *Greater Manchester Transport Society*

Vol. 5   NOVEMBER/DECEMBER, 1951   No. 4

THE NOR-WESTER

Compliments of the Season

From the Chairman :

I SEND to each and everyone connected with the North Western Company my sincere good wishes for a Merry Xmas and a Happy New Year. I hope in January to have the opportunity of meeting some of you at the Long Service Presentation. The fact that this year our numbers have grown to such an extent that they are too great to have all the past and present recipients at the one function and yet preserve the intimate atmosphere of past years, is some indication of the number of Old Stalwarts with us today. My especial greetings to the over "twenty-fives."

           J. W. WOMAR.

From the Managing Director :

A T the close of each year we are apt to remember the unpleasant rather than the pleasant events of the past twelve months. With the commencement of the New Year we look forward instinctively for better things.

Let us hope that 1952 will see the fulfilment of at any rate some of our aspirations and that it will prove to be the turning point in our post war experiences.

Cheerfulness in the face of difficulties and the determination to give of one's best are infectious and often produce results far beyond one's expectations.

I send to all my sincere greetings for Christmas and Best Wishes for a Happy New Year.

           T. R. WILLIAMS.

Restrictions on paper and printing-ink supplies were still in force in 1951, but that December's edition of the staff magazine made the best of what was available. *Ian Yearsley*

No 432, a Willowbrook-rebodied Bristol K5G of 1939, and all-Leyland PD2 224 of 1948, in their original livery were typical double-deckers of the company's final 'glory days' of the 1950s. Fortunately both are now preserved, being seen here at a recent Trans-Lancs Rally. *Author*

usually appear in the procession, fully decorated. For King George V's Silver Jubilee in 1935 the company surpassed itself by festooning a newly rebodied Tilling saloon with more than 2,000 light bulbs, fed by banks of 12-volt batteries which displaced virtually all the seating. The bus visited all districts in turn, depot inspectors being required to prepare advertised routes for it to be seen by the largest possible audience throughout their territory. The exercise was repeated two years later for the 1937 Coronation.

North Western, then, was a company embracing virtually the whole range of bus and coach operation, from intensive urban services to sparse rural ones. Although municipal operators generally offered better conditions of service, staff were attracted by greater overtime opportunities, the variety of work (even on stage-carriage duties) and a chance to work on long-distance express services and private hires. Social clubs were fostered at every garage, and team spirit developed further

through a welfare society and, postwar, a staff magazine, *The Nor' Wester*.

The ultimate private hire was the charter of Dennis Loline 814 for a trip to Moscow by Manchester University Students' Union members in the mid-1960s. The interior was specially adapted, and the company sensibly provided two drivers and a fitter who had done National Service in West Germany. More mundane were the many 'fishing parties', which typically set out at around 11pm on a Friday, travelled a significant distance, and returned at about 1am on the Sunday, during which drivers had great difficulty in complying with their Hours Regulations, beyond napping on the back seat of their coach on the Saturday. The other regular alternative was the 'breakfast party', a euphemism for drinking out-of-hours. These went to one of many country pubs not so far afield, like the 'Red Lion' at Pickmere or 'The Gun' at Hollingworth, with capacity for about 40 diners. They commenced picking-up around 6am, usually in the less-affluent districts of Manchester, and headed for a 'Full English Breakfast' at their chosen hostelry. Under contemporary licensing laws the alcoholic drinks permitted for consumption with a meal were stretched out until 'opening hours' from around noon to 3pm. After an extended post-lunch 'drinking-up time' the return journey finally commenced at about 4pm!

Licences were also held for 'Extended Tours', but in practice these were operated only on behalf of Co-operative Travel Services as eight-day events for pensioners in the months of April, May, June, and September, when hotels were cheaper, and coaches available.

The company's dismemberment in 1972, solely for being in the wrong place at the wrong time, brought an unjust end to a long and fine heritage. However, I sincerely hope that these pages fire the reader's interest and truly reflect the 'glory days' of this once-great company.

Ted Jones
Church Stretton
February 2008

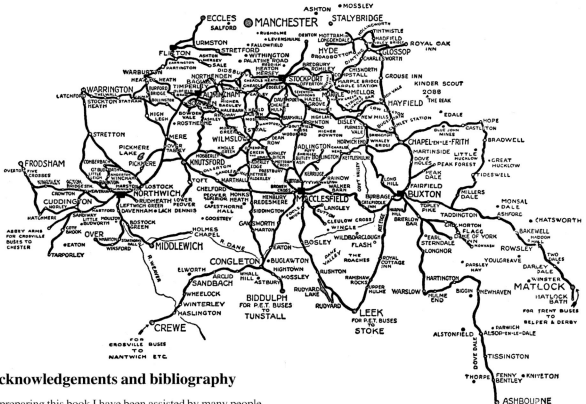

The remarkable development of North Western's network, just before the 1928 extensions into central Manchester, and with only a tenuous connection with Flixton. The detached operations from Oldham garage are depicted on page 15.

Acknowledgements and bibliography

In preparing this book I have been assisted by many people but particularly Peter Caunt and David Pickup, who provided considerable information from experience in working for the company. Among others who made their records available were Peter Waller (Ian Allan Publishing), Dennis Talbot and George Turnbull (Greater Manchester Transport Society), Alan Mills (The Omnibus Society), Peter Jaques (Kithead Trust) and Geoff Lumb. Many more provided photographs for consideration, notably Michael Eyre, Dennis Gill, John Hillmer, Martin Jenkins (Online Transport Archive), Tony Moyes, Monica Richardson (Photobus), Peter Roberts, Colin Routh, John Senior, Ken Swallow and Peter Thompson (Photosales), while yet others no less helpful are credited in the captions; my thanks to all of you — and to anyone inadvertently omitted! Every effort has been made to trace the provenance of the photographs used, but this has not proved possible in every case; sincere apologies are offered for any omissions or incorrect attributions, in which event the author should be contacted via the publisher. My gratitude is due also to Chris Heaps, Bruce Maund and, once again, Michael Eyre, all of whom provided further valuable information while checking and correcting the manuscript. Some of the statistics and fleet details quoted come from General Manager's Reports, while others are from the PSV Circle's comprehensive Fleet History (2PC3); where these sources differed I have tended to rely on the former. Much more could have been written had not space precluded it, and readers seeking greater detail are advised to consult the two-volume history of the company, edited by Eric Ogden and published in 1980/1 by the Transport Publishing Company.

1. Infancy

At the dawn of the 20th century the British Electric Traction Company, founded in 1896, was busy building power stations and commissioning electric-supply systems throughout the United Kingdom, mostly in urban districts where local authorities had not yet taken any such action, bearing in mind that this period was still the infancy of public electricity supply. To create a useful electricity base-load it was soon promoting, building and operating electric tramway systems, being the largest group engaged in this activity. Other promoters were also in action, to the extent that between 1895 and 1905 there was something of a 'tramway mania'. As had been the case with the 'railway mania' of the 1840s the bubble burst, at least for companies, due to rooted objection, insufficient finance, lack of commercial viability and, with tramways, unreasonable local-authority demands for highway improvements.

Well aware of the way the wind was blowing, BET decided to focus on areas with promising potential, without incurring the heavy investment necessary for tramway infrastructure. This started in a very tentative way with the supply, as early as April 1901, of two Straker-Squire steam buses to the group's Potteries Electric Traction Co, an operation which lasted scarcely 12 months due to inadequate technology. Further attempts with motor buses were made in 1904 by PET and by a Birmingham & Midland Motor Omnibus Co subsidiary, neither faring much better. The potential benefits were there to see, however, and a subsidiary, the British Automobile Development Company, was formed in 1905. From *c*1910 the group's involvement with buses became more extensive, as proven innovations like petrol-electric propulsion offered a practical alternative to still-frail mechanical transmissions. By 1912, renamed as the British Automobile Traction Company (better BAT than BAD), it was well into fostering bus operations as 'stand-alone' operations as well as

feeder services to existing tramways. Having identified promising 'tramless' territories, BET delegated individual directors to survey their potential, and Sidney Garcke (the son of BET founder Emil Garcke), who had established Deal & District Motor Services in Kent, was charged with 'prospecting' the Macclesfield district in Cheshire.

A Macclesfield & District Tramways Co had obtained a Parliamentary Act in 1906 to build a direct line to Hazel Grove to meet Stockport's municipal system. Connections had also been authorised to others from Poynton towards Bramhall, Cheadle and Wilmslow, none of which materialised, apart from a short Stockport extension in Hazel Grove to the 'Rising Sun' junction in 1911. In that same year there was an attempt to bring trolley-buses to Macclesfield, when an Act of Parliament was applied for, but then withdrawn, by the awkwardly titled Macclesfield & District Railless Electric Traction & Electricity Supply Co.

BAT therefore had a clear field to start operations around the town on 10 November 1913, apart from difficulties in getting licences to ply for hire from some local authorities. Services were soon established to Cheadle (Cheshire) via Monks Heath and Wilmslow (directly replacing a long-established horse-bus service through a largely rural catchment area), to Buxton via the 'Cat & Fiddle' and to Leek via Rudyard. On these three routes alone BAT's buses were running 1,200 miles daily by May 1914. Further services were started to Congleton and thence to Biddulph or to Crewe via Sandbach and to Bollington, as well as to Altrincham via Prestbury and Wilmslow. The BAT livery was green and cream, and the single-deck Daimler buses bore 'British' on their side panels, the local operation having been designated the BAT Co Ltd (Macclesfield Branch).

These new services soon attracted patronage, once people got over their reluctance to journey beyond traditional bounds, and on mechanical contrivances. All too soon there was a dramatic downturn, with the outbreak of World War 1 in August 1914, a mere nine months after operations had started. Many chassis were requisitioned by the Army, staff left to 'join the colours', passengers volunteered to join the Armed Forces, and relatively little war work was allocated to local manufacturers in this centre of the British silk industry. Substitute chassis were obtained, by definition of types not robust enough for Army service, but the company could not take advantage of licences granted by Altrincham in April 1915, although a service to Cheadle started that September to meet wartime needs. Operations were severely curtailed, and those to Leek, Buxton and Altrincham were suspended altogether by October 1916. Even the Macclesfield–Crewe service was curtailed to Congleton for two years from February 1917, due to petrol shortages.

In 1919 the company took up the baton again and concentrated on getting services back on the road, as soon as it could obtain AEC and Daimler chassis, some of which received stored prewar bodies. The Macclesfield–Altrincham service was not amongst them for a while, and some others were no longer daily. At the helm was a new local manager, George Cardwell, who prior to Army service had gained considerable experience in pioneering bus operations for other BET-group companies. His astute and positive personality would ensure that expansion became the keynote to success, and it was probably his inspiration to approach Stockport Corporation in July 1919, seeking to run a Macclesfield service directly into the town. Stockport consented only if 3d (1.25p) per mile were paid for road repairs and the service routed via Offerton, a district served from March 1913 to June 1919 by one of the earliest trolleybus operations in the UK (intended to reach Marple), for which replacement motor buses

were on order. BAT agreed to the diversion but refused to pay the levy. The resultant stalemate was soon broken by chance, as a National Railway Strike erupted on 29 September 1919, and the town's Watch (i.e. Police) Committee was directed by the Home Office to issue licences to BAT for through services from Stockport to Buxton, to Macclesfield and to Warrington via Altrincham, to mitigate its effects. It was a fleeting victory, however, as the company withdrew all these services just nine weeks later after threats of legal action for road-maintenance charges from the Cheshire and Derbyshire county councils, in addition to Stockport Corporation.

Belatedly, in January 1920 Stockport's Watch Committee sought advice from the Tramways Committee about BAT's approach, the upshot being conditions that (a) BAT should charge a 75% fare premium on routes which overlapped those of the Corporation, (b) no more than four return journeys per day should be operated on any single service without specific permission, and (c) the road-maintenance charges would still apply. The company agreed to the first, as it had no intention of competing for local traffic, noted the second but stated that it planned to operate more than four journeys per day on all its services, and rejected the third, which, it maintained, it could not afford unless the charge were paid retrospectively (i.e. on actual rather than forecast mileage). The Corporation would not accept this, and BAT asked for a six-month waiver, by which time imminent changes in motor taxation might be clarified.

Although the 'Stockport situation' remained unresolved, developments continued apace. By the summer of 1920 ten

One of the infant operation's earliest buses taking a breather at the 'Cat & Fiddle' Inn between Buxton and Macclesfield, at 1,772ft (540m) above sea level the highest in England. Situated on a ridge separating Cheshire and Derbyshire and bedevilled by hostile weather, it represented a terrific challenge for such early buses, if not more so for the horse-drawn wagonette ahead. *Geoff Lumb collection*

A 1921 addition to the 'British'
ranks, MA 7485 (No 391,
later 43) bears an AEC radiator
(although recorded as a
Daimler), had Brush 29-seat
bodywork, and gave a
creditable eight years' service.
Dennis Gill collection

services were being advertised, including new ones from
Macclesfield to Knutsford via Chelford, to New Mills via Hazel
Grove (worked through as an extension of the Macclesfield–
Hazel Grove service) and all-day through-working between
Cheadle and Buxton, creating a 26-mile route. Additionally three
town services were started in Buxton on a very 'thin' timetable.
The indirect service to New Mills seems an unlikely development
but generated traffic with Stockport from two directions in
connecting with the Corporation's trams and also established
a foothold on the A6 towards Buxton.

In addition to regular stopping services — frequently adjusted
to optimise net revenue — an ambitious programme of excursions
was offered from Macclesfield, running as far as Rhyl, Southport
and Blackpool, though fares of 18s (90p) were not cheap in
relation to average wages of well under £3 a week. However,
closer attractions at more-affordable fares were not overlooked,
these including Chatsworth House and Castleton. Meanwhile,
fine-tuning was taking place all the time; the service to Knutsford
via Chelford started in July 1920 with just two return journeys
a day, only to be suspended eight weeks later. Likewise the

longer-established service to Leek had been adjusted in July
to operate three round-trips on Wednesdays and Saturdays, two
sufficing for the rest of the week, and in winter the third trip
was eliminated altogether.

In May 1920 BAT had applied to Stockport for permission to
run to Cheadle Hulme via Adswood and to Altrincham via
Didsbury, although how that secured Manchester's agreement is a
mystery, as it ran across much more of the latter's territory, albeit
less developed then. Stockport Corporation restated its previous
conditions, but BAT kept its powder dry by not responding,
aware that new legislation due to come into force on 1 January
1921 would prevent the granting of licences to ply for hire being
conditional on payment of road-maintenance charges! In the
meantime it announced that it was actively seeking local
garaging. By Christmas 1920 Buxton had gained recognition on
timetable covers as an operating centre, a small garage at
Burbage providing buses for the clutch of town services radiating
from the railway station, still at sparse frequencies. However, the
service via the 'Cat & Fiddle' had been reduced to three return
journeys on Mondays, Wednesdays, Saturdays, and Sundays

only, 'fog and snow permitting'. Excursions were still offered from Macclesfield to less-distant locations, but experience dictated that they were subject to cancellation if fewer than 25 seats had been booked.

The company bided its time until January 1921, when Stockport got its BAT service through Offerton, but not in the manner envisaged, as this materialised as a through route via Marple to New Mills. Services were also started to Buxton via Whaley Bridge, to Macclesfield direct and, more locally, to Bramhall via Davenport. Probably due to vehicle shortage, those from Macclesfield to Altrincham and to Knutsford and from Knutsford via High Legh to Latchford (Warrington boundary) remained 'temporarily suspended'. The new Stockport services brought a confusing reallocation of route numbers, about which BAT (and, later, North Western) was quite cavalier. Fortunately these were not then displayed on the buses, but they did appear in the public timetables, without a word of warning or explanation! The March 1921 timetable was the first to bear the imprint 'Macclesfield, Buxton and Stockport Districts', and by the fourth quarter of the year Stockport had become the magnet, more passengers being carried on routes based on the town than the combined total on all other services. During the year Stockport Corporation displayed a streak of generosity in temporarily garaging four company vehicles, for a modest charge.

Developments continued unabated, and by December 1922 no fewer than 22 basic services were being operated, some via alternative routes. Since March of that year the Stockport–New Mills service had been extended to Hayfield, and in April a further service was added to Wilmslow via Bramhall. Buxton was now operating longer-distance connections to Leek, Matlock Bath, Ashbourne and to Glossop via Hayfield, 'weather conditions permitting' — not that those to Leek over Axe Edge, and to Ashbourne along the Via Gellia (A515) were easy going! During the winter, excursions were limited to 'away games of all Macclesfield [football] clubs'. There were some strange anomalies, however, the Leek timetable offering connections with Potteries buses to Hanley, although there were no timetabled BAT journeys south of Bosley that winter! Likewise the Buxton–Matlock Bath service required passengers to change at Bakewell on all journeys. On the other hand the Altrincham–Stockport service was linked through to Buxton.

Bigger changes were afoot, however, as by mid-1922 only the 'Macclesfield Branch' was still administered directly by BAT from London, and at that late date a special 'Peak District Committee'

of directors was delegated for this task. During that year, quite coincidentally, another major force in the bus industry, the London-based Thomas Tilling Group, acquired a significant shareholding in BAT, and as this was not considered a hostile development, the advantage must have been to increase funds for expansion. Amongst the first fruits was the registration on 23 April 1923 of the Macclesfield operation as a public company, with a nominal capital of £100,000, in which the two groups had an equal investment. The name chosen was 'North Western Road Car Co Ltd', the Registered Office remaining for the time being at King Edward Street, Macclesfield. Continuity in management was assured by the appointment of Sidney Garcke as a director and of George Cardwell as General Manager, whilst the first Chairman was BET director W. S. Wreathall, also Chairman of Ribble Motor Services and a well-known pioneer in the bus industry. Other directors were C. S. B. Hilton, of Eastern Counties Road Car, and Walter Wolsey and G. Wolsey, both Thomas Tilling men. Perhaps the most visible sign of the new order was a radical change of livery, green giving way to red as the principal colour.

Believed to be ex-War Office in 1920, XB 9978 was a Daimler Y acquired via BAT to bolster the new company's fleet strength in May 1923. Initially numbered 451, then 63 (from 1927), it would be withdrawn in 1928. It too had a 29-seat Brush body, seen here in North Western's red and white livery. Note the unpainted aluminium scuttle, a fleet characteristic throughout most of the decade. *Senior Transport Archive*

2. Growing Pains

Mid-Cheshire No 5, a rare
35hp Enfield with 30-seat
body, dating from 1914,
was acquired as a runner
upon takeover of that firm
in January 1925 but was not
operated by North Western.
*Cheshire & Chester Archives
& Local Studies*

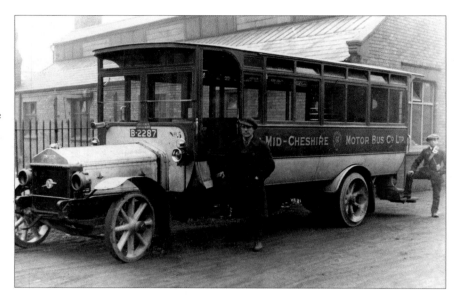

▶ With continual service developments
the new board decided to move the
company's headquarters to Stockport,
which demonstrably offered greater
potential, having generated 1.5 million
passenger journeys during 1922.
Accordingly, a new garage/workshop
site was selected on the south side of the
town, in Charles Street off Higher
Hillgate, which was occupied in 1924,
with open parking for the initial
allocation. By March 1924 the fleet
amounted to 73 buses and seven
charabancs, comprising AEC and
Daimler chassis, which had run
1,580,000 miles in just 12 months,
carrying five million passengers, and
300 staff were on the payroll.

Anticipating the move to Stockport,
North Western sought a better working
relationship with its new host town,
which had a modest but flourishing
tramway system connecting directly with that of Manchester
Corporation in the town centre (!) and also at Reddish (Bull's
Head) and with the Stalybridge, Hyde, Mossley & Dukinfield
Joint Board's system at Pole Bank, Woodley, on a route to Hyde.
The tracks for the first couple of miles over the direct route to the
city lay in Heaton Norris, which, as a separate authority in 1902,
had leased them to Manchester upon electrification, as successor
to the through Manchester Carriage & Tramways Co's horse-car
service. Along Stockport's major route, south to Hazel Grove,
BAT's new services undoubtedly creamed off some traffic.
Stockport was further disconcerted when North Western applied
in January 1923 for a service to Denton, partially overlapping
the Hyde tram route, and therefore sought compensatory annual
payments. Almost certainly mindful of the effect of unrestricted
bus competition on BET's tramway investments elsewhere, the
North Western directors offered from £150 to £300 per annum in

respect of net profits earned in the town, the precise figure each
year to be determined by the ratio of the length of services within
the borough to the total length of all the company's services.

Consent was given for the Denton service, but only with an
'off-centre' town terminus at Andrew Square, instead of the
Mersey Square focus of most other bus and tram services.
The company reluctantly accepted this situation and within 12
months was also running to Mellor via Bredbury, albeit finding
the lack of easy interchange (and the supervision of services
from separated termini) problematic, to say the least. Stockport
suggested it might allow the two new services to terminate in
Mersey Square if buses did not exceed 6mph over the 'gap'; prior
to 1940 the two locations were linked by only two busy, narrow
thoroughfares, Underbank/Chestergate or Princes Street, the
latter used by intensive tram services over single-line and loop
tracks. The company elected to leave things as they were!

As 1924 dawned North Western attempted to project its trunk services from Stockport into Manchester but was refused by the city's Watch Committee, which did not want to compromise its refusal to allow even its own Corporation's buses into the central area, on grounds of heavy traffic congestion already caused by tramcars.

Further afield, territory for development was staked out by two strategic purchases. The first, in November 1924, was the Mid-Cheshire Motor Bus Co of Northwich, which had been registered in January 1914 by Thomas Wilkinson, a local man. Whilst having infrequent services to towns as distant as Warrington and Sandbach, much of its work consisted of unpublicised factory services around Northwich for the many employees of Brunner, Mond & Co (soon to become a major constituent of ICI Ltd). Mid-Cheshire was also developing services around Flixton, Stretford, Eccles and Patricroft on the western edge of Manchester, a dormitory area for workers in Trafford Park, home to Ford Motor Co, British Westinghouse and many other major enterprises. It has been said that Mid-Cheshire was snatched literally overnight from under Crosville's nose, which had been in the midst of joint discussions with North Western

for its acquisition against a rival bid from Altrincham & District Motor Bus Services Ltd. The latter was a subsidiary of John Wood & Son Ltd, a furniture-removals company which had put its first bus on the road in August 1921. On the other hand, J. Crosland-Taylor's version was that Mid-Cheshire held out for too high a price from Crosville, but one that George Cardwell was prepared to pay. Perhaps that is how he preferred to recall it!

North Western alleged that Altrincham & District had become a thorn in its side in competing aggressively on several key services it was trying to establish, one from Altrincham to Stockport via Gatley being particularly provocative. This is a moot point, however, for BAT/North Western might sometimes have been considered the aggressor. However, in December 1925 Altrincham & District succumbed to the blandishments of North Western's directors. Both A&D and Mid-Cheshire had less than 30 buses each and probably needed more investment capital, but their acquisition added some good vehicles, three garages

A Daimler Y type, Mid-Cheshire No 52 had already been replaced by a new Leyland before the North Western takeover and was possibly an ex-WD chassis which failed to perform. The high-mounted charabanc body looks like a weekend alternative to a saloon. The photograph was taken at Park Green, Macclesfield, in 1920. *Cheshire & Chester Archives & Local Studies*

A contemporary trade advertisement portraying a 1920 Mid-Cheshire Leyland 36hp new in the early 1920s. The destination display might be a mock-up, but its clarity would put most of today's equivalents to shame. *Author's collection*

13

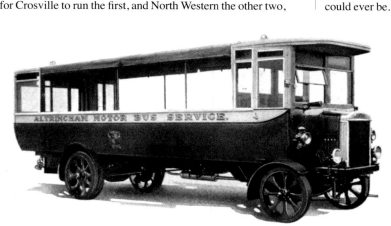

and useful services in the rapidly
developing Timperley, Sale, Urmston,
Flixton and Davyhulme districts, in
addition to those radiating from Northwich
and Altrincham. Incidentally, A&D had
earned praise for a policy of employing
one-armed ex-World War 1 servicemen as
conductors, at least one of them remaining
on the staff at Altrincham beyond 1945. Its
well-maintained fleet was largely of
Leyland manufacture, leavened by a heady
mixture of 14-seater charabancs for hires
and local excursions.

Relationships with Crosville were not
affected too badly, as North Western was
able to gain agreement to a boundary
starting at Warrington and running via
Frodsham, Delamere, Vale Royal,
Winsford, Middlewich and Sandbach to Congleton and Biddulph.
In the same year (1925) Lancashire United accepted the
Manchester Ship Canal as a boundary from Warrington to
Manchester. In all these cases, rights to existing anomalies were
preserved, such as penetrations to natural traffic objectives like
Trafford Park and Flixton (LUT), Northwich and Frodsham–
Warrington (Crosville) and Eccles, Chester, Runcorn and Crewe
(NWRCC). There was further agreement in 1931 over nominally
joint services to the last three, as it was felt to be more economic
for Crosville to run the first, and North Western the other two,

with a few specified journeys by the alternative operator. Such
had been the mutual concern in the early days of joint working
that passengers between Northwich and Chester were made
to change buses at Vale Royal (Abbey Arms)! Some of these
area agreements were due to the influence of Sidney Garcke,
since 1923 Chairman of the whole Tilling-BAT group,
who believed strongly that territories mutually recognised
by the larger operators were a far better way to build a
sustainable network than dangerous cut-throat competition
could ever be.

Entry to Warrington was gained by an
agreement dated 19 January 1925. This
allowed passengers to travel between Thelwall
('Dog & Dart') or Stretton ('Cat & Lion')
and the town centre only on payment of
double the tram fare from town to Latchford
or Stockton Heath tram termini, however short
their journey, the tram-fare equivalent being
remitted to the Corporation. Warrington, like
Stockport, was going to be a long-running saga.

On the opposite side of its territory
North Western was stung into action by a
Ribble attempt in 1924 to infiltrate the Pennine
flanks beyond Oldham with a service to Elland
via Denshaw and Buckstones Moor, which was
denied the necessary licences. North Western

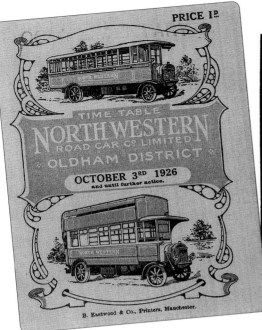

PRICE 1D.

TIME TABLE
NORTH WESTERN
ROAD CAR CO LIMITED
OLDHAM DISTRICT

OCTOBER 3RD 1926
and until further notice.

B. Eastwood & Co., Printers, Manchester.

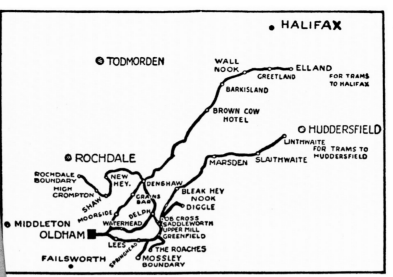

Before 1929 these services were operated from Oldham garage in isolation from the rest of the network on page 7.

promptly moved into some of the townships beyond the tentacles of the Oldham and SHMD Board tramways with a two-way circular service from Oldham via Scouthead, Delph, Uppermill, and Lees. By 1927 quite a network had been opened up in the district, courtesy of co-ordination with Oldham. A northerly projection from Newhey via Shaw to the Rochdale boundary at Springfield Mills was soon operated jointly with that authority, being through-worked from 1927, but North Western would never have more than a tenuous connection with the town.

In 1926 well-equipped workshops were commissioned at Charles Street, enabling a consistent maintenance regime to be established, with local garage servicing at 3,000-mile intervals interspersed with heavy docking at Stockport every 9,000 miles. Unit replacement was instituted of mechanical items as large as complete engines, and bodies were overhauled

One of 24 Tilling-Stevens TS6 petrol-electrics delivered in 1925 with 51-seat Tilling bodywork and withdrawn in 1930/1, No 179 subsequently became a showman's vehicle, but around a dozen of its sisters spent most of the 1930s providing staff transport for Chivers' Jams in Cambridgeshire; of these a lone example survived to be rescued for preservation and, restored to its former glory, can nowadays be seen at the Greater Manchester Transport Society's museum.
Senior Transport Archive

The double-deckers had been preceded in 1924 by 37 Tilling-Stevens 36-seater saloons, the first with Stockport registrations, and the driver of No 85, 'fag' dangling during a layover in Buxton on a Matlock duty, must have hoped that higher authority wouldn't see this picture! The lower profile of the cab roof suggests that the canopy of a double-deck body would fit neatly over it, body interchange being common practice at this time. *Stockport Local Heritage Library*

With a more conventional Tilling full-canopy body and neater destination display in the windscreen, 1925 Tilling-Stevens saloon No 162 had an extensive canvas-covered roof opening and was an early example of fleet and registration number alignment. The unequally sized front and rear wheels suggest a recent conversion from solid tyres, which may explain why this photograph was discovered in discarded archives of the West Yorkshire Road Car Co, another keen operator of the marque. *C. W. Routh collection*

and repainted annually, often emerging on different chassis. This resulted in the double-deckers' not being restricted to their original 'mounts' and body numbering in a separate series 1,000 higher than the externally displayed fleet numbers — a practice which was to continue until the late-1940s, long after the need had vanished. By March 1927 fleet strength for the 83 stage-carriage services in operation had reached 208, comprising 35 Daimlers, 25 AECs and 110 new Tilling-Stevens, as well as acquired Leylands (26), Renaults (10) and De Dions (2); annual ridership amounted to 21 million journeys, over 700 miles of route.

In July 1926 North Western successfully revived Ribble's aspirations across the moors to Elland, although the full service was run only at weekends, being otherwise restricted to Oldham–Denshaw. Subsequently the Elland journeys were extended to Halifax by this indirect route, but traffic was too sparse for it to survive beyond February 1928. Meanwhile, the company sought further expansion directly towards both Huddersfield and Halifax. For the former, starting early in 1925, the service was limited initially to Saddleworth–Marsden on weekdays, but at weekends it ran from Oldham as far as the Huddersfield boundary at Linthwaite. Huddersfield refused to licence an extension into the town centre for another three years, until it made the error of submitting a Parliamentary Bill to run Corporation motor buses outside the borough (its trams had been running the 7½ miles out to Marsden since 1914). Warned by its Parliamentary Agent, North Western immediately lodged an objection, duly gaining the desired result of an agreement to run into the town, subject to protection for local services. Accordingly the local service from Oldham was replaced on 29 March 1929 by a through service from Manchester to Huddersfield, the precursor of much more ambitious plans for a service from Liverpool to Newcastle upon Tyne.

Halifax was a different scenario, in that in April 1926 North Western initiated a stopping service from Oldham via Denshaw and Ripponden, in direct opposition to an 'express' pioneered the previous year by Ripponden & District Motor Services, and only a month or so before the latter was extended into Manchester. Twelve months later Oldham Corporation joined forces with North Western but in July 1928 incurred the displeasure of West Riding County Council over potential road wear after applying to run three-axle double-deckers, being reminded that it had powers to run only five miles beyond its boundaries. Thereafter North Western carried on alone beyond Denshaw, converting the service to limited-stop status and in May 1929 extending it

through to Manchester. It was soon joined by BET-owned Yorkshire Woollen District, the service being extended in Yorkshire to Bradford. This continued to run in competition with Ripponden & District, which had also reached Bradford on the 'return-ticket' principle (through refusal of local licences) but would be cut back again after the two major companies offered a co-ordination agreement in 1931 at the Traffic Commissioners' behest; R&D's express service was eventually bought out in September 1936. The latter continued to run some local bus services for a little longer — and excursions and tours until 1957 — and still exists today as a successful regional parcels-carrier.

Back in August 1926 Halifax and Rochdale corporations had started a through service over Blackstone Edge, but Rochdale was left to carry on alone after February 1928, though not for long; it had to cease that December, again due to County Council interference, whereupon North Western tried to pick up the reins but was in turn rebuffed, LMS Railway Road Services succeeding under a 'Railways (Road Powers) Act', of which more anon. The service eventually became a Hebble operation, in which North Western was invited to participate but declined on being required to pay 10% of gross receipts earned between Littleborough and Rochdale.

At Glossop the local eight-car tramway, owned by the Urban Electric Supply Co Ltd, was abandoned on Christmas Eve 1927, and North Western gained great credit by starting a replacement bus service at short notice, from Boxing Day. Although this was done at the Town Council's behest, and the company was already running in from Buxton and Marple Bridge, the authority acted with very bad grace in taking three months to grant long-term licences, because of potential interest shown by the Glossop Carriage Co, which had failed to rise to the initial emergency.

In April 1927 Manchester's forward-looking General Manager, Henry Mattinson, initiated a network of limited-stop bus services at premium fares, co-ordinated with neighbouring operators to provide cross-city connections between many towns on the periphery, although the first experiment, from Cheadle to Heywood via Wilmslow Road and Rochdale Road, was started by the Corporation alone. The intention was to protect the municipal tramways from emerging private operators, amongst which North Western was by far the largest. The company quickly realised that its survival was in jeopardy, its inter-urban routes being held at bay at Cheadle, Stockport and Altrincham from the natural traffic objective of the city centre. However, in its firmness Manchester was fair and objective, allowing any

Bell Punch 'Bellgraphic' ticket used as common stock on Tyne–Tees–Mersey services by all operators from the mid-1930s. These were handwritten by the conductor on the top plate of the machine, which retained a copy for audit.

operator which had a well-defined territory and accepted the standard terms of the 'Co-ordinated Motor Bus Network' agreement to join in. North Western applied and was accepted, joining the scheme for cross-city services on 8 March 1928. None of the municipal operators saw benefit in running far out into Cheshire and Derbyshire, and so under a parallel 'By Agreement' formula, involving lump-sum rather than mileage-related payments, Manchester also allowed the company's Buxton, Hayfield, Macclesfield, Higher Poynton and Bramhall services to run into the city centre from 1 March 1928. The new spirit of co-operation did see Manchester's buses briefly running as far out as Handforth from 30 June, however.

An unwanted side-effect was police pressure for new city terminal facilities, to reduce central-area congestion, and a project already underway was appropriated for the purpose. Unfortunately it was located distinctly off-centre, in the shadow of Central station (today's 'Manchester Central', also known as 'G-Mex') and a tedious walk from the main shopping area and commercial district. The site was that of today's Bridgewater Hall and had to be brought into use for the medium-distance services extended into the city, although construction of facilities had barely begun! Its intended role for express services had been evidenced by its incorporation four months earlier as a separate company, Omnibus Stations Ltd, funded by a consortium of nine Tilling-BAT companies and Lancashire United, as potential express-coach operators from the city; North Western and Ribble subscribed £12,500 each, the other eight much less. Its Secretary held the same post with North Western, whose General Manager held a seat on the board, and the registered office was at Charles Street, although all administrative staff were based at the new facility.

The Co-ordinated Services scheme had got into its stride from January 1928, and amongst many links were Urmston–Rochdale in February (extended a month later as Flixton–Bacup), Gatley–Shaw/Scouthead in March (extended in May to Uppermill), Flixton–Stalybridge, also in March, and Chorlton–Stalybridge in February 1929 (extended that May to Glossop, with North Western participation). This took some pressure off Lower Mosley Street, which was sorely needed for its intended purpose and would be further relieved in the early 1930s by the opening of Parker Street (Piccadilly) bus station. However, the company did not participate in all these services at any one time, there being regular adjustment to balance spheres of operation, mileage and revenue. For example, North Western's entitlement in the

Flixton–Bacup service was offset against a greater share of other Manchester–Flixton joint services.

The opening of Lower Mosley Street on 8 March 1928 was also a precursor to a significant increase in long-distance coach operation by the company, applications having been lodged with the city's Watch Committee for 19 express services in all directions other than to Scotland and the North West of England, which beyond Bolton and Wigan was to be exclusively Ribble territory, apart from services to Liverpool, Southport and Blackpool. Not all could be started, however, due to the refusal of licences by some local authorities. The famous express services to Blackpool, joint with Ribble and Lancashire United, finally commenced on 8 July 1928, after North Western had been operating independently for almost two months. North Western had a 25% share of the timetable and received from Ribble $\frac{2}{7}$ of the revenue collected in the Ribble area, whilst Lancashire United had to pay North Western $\frac{3}{11}$ of the revenue collected between Manchester and Bolton or Wingates (Westhoughton)!

In March 1929 limited-stop services started simultaneously to Huddersfield and Liverpool on a co-ordinated timetable,

North Western running to the latter via Altrincham, and Lancashire United via Eccles, to overcome intermediate licensing objections. Two months later, services began to Derby, Nottingham, Halifax, Barnsley and Castleton (for Sheffield), and the Huddersfield service was extended to Leeds and Newcastle. By that summer there were diverging services beyond Leeds to Scarborough, Bridlington and Hull, five area-agreement operators were contributing vehicles and crews, and through bookings were offered to all major points to and from the Liverpool services. On 2 August a service was also started via Birmingham and Oxford to London, operated jointly with BMMO ('Midland Red') and offering bookable connections to Aberystwyth, South Wales and the South West, which objectives had been denied the previous year as destinations for direct services. To cope with all this a Manchester garage was opened off Chester Road, about a mile from Lower Mosley Street.

Other significant moves were afoot and, as the decade ended, North Western reached an agreement on its operating area with the London, Midland & Scottish and London & North Eastern railways, which largely tallied with the Area Agreements fostered by Sidney Garcke. This arose through Parliamentary Acts obtained in August 1928 by each of the four main-line railway companies to operate bus services on a wider scale. Whereas some had operated buses in their own names, they now preferred to invest in existing groups such as Tilling, BAT, BET, National Omnibus (later Eastern, Southern and Western National) and some significant independents, such as Hebble and Crosville. They also set up joint committees with municipalities running longer-distance services, achieved only in Yorkshire's West Riding. Their investment was very welcome to some of the companies affected but gave a hostage to fortune in granting railway representation on the boards of their new 'business partners'. This major development spurred the Tilling and BAT groups to form a common holding company for those operators in which both had shareholdings, although some important BET companies remained outside the arrangement, without

railway involvement. Under this new regime North Western came under Tilling control, and in April 1930 the LMS and LNER acquired equal minority shareholdings.

Despite the new arrangements there would be battles with the railways for many years to come, over express services, their duplication and even shorter-distance connections, whenever railway interests were threatened. In North Western's case railway blessing was gained for access to Huddersfield, Halifax, and Sheffield, where railway part-ownership of municipal operations had just been effected. Operating boundaries were also agreed amicably with Trent Motor Traction and East Midland Motor Services, but discussions with entrenched fellow companies Yorkshire Traction (at Huddersfield), Yorkshire Woollen District (at Halifax) and Ribble (in Rochdale) were more protracted, agreement not being reached until December 1930.

The 1920s could truly be said to have been 'glory days' in the most heroic sense, for the fleet had grown from fewer than 25 to nearly 300 buses and by 1930 was almost completely standardised on Tilling-Stevens chassis, with Tilling or Brush bodywork. The few exceptions were 25 new Leyland Tigers and six early-model Leylands and AECs acquired in 1928 with the business of Flixton-based Tetlow & Collier.

The majority of the Tilling-Stevens were B10A Express models with straight mechanical transmission, but a dozen were B9As, which were more economical on fuel, probably on account of differing transmission characteristics. However, the first 98 were petrol-electrics dating from 1924 to 1926, which averaged about 4-5mpg but could return as little as 3mpg, depending on condition and terrain, 24 having outside-staircase open-top double-deck bodywork. Some of the saloons had as part of their roofs roll-up canvas covers, which garage staff had to nail down during gusty weather in exposed areas. In 1927 more than half the fleet (by then already 200 strong) had been converted to run on pneumatic tyres.

By March 1930 the number of services had increased from eight to 112 (in 9¼ years), covered 1,417 route miles, over which

◄ Eighty more B10As, with better destination displays and fixed roofs, were commissioned in 1929. No 333 would have its 36-seat Tilling body replaced by a new half-canopy Eastern Counties one in 1935, thereby seeing out the war years. Some of this batch were also withdrawn as early as 1934 and sold to sister companies, others being requisitioned or loaned to Crosville during the war, but even those that lasted to 1946 saw further service elsewhere following sale to dealers, some, heavily disguised, lasting into the early 1950s. *Greater Manchester Transport Society*

11,558,000 vehicle miles had been run in the previous 12 months from nine garages, catering for 36,333,000 passenger journeys (compared with 546,000 in 1919/20), and 283 buses were owned. Annual revenue had increased to £542,000 (comparable figures not having been published for the BAT era), and the company had been transformed from a struggling local independent to become a soundly based major regional undertaking, achieving a 10% dividend on its ordinary shares by 1929 and, by dint of a special bonus, declaring 20% for the 12 months ending 31 March 1930!

◄ One of the potent-looking Leyland Tigers bought for the new London service in 1929, the comprehensive route information displaying a 'LIMITED STOP' rather than an 'EXPRESS' designation, as was North Western's practice for some years. Nevertheless, No 405 looked more like a chopped-down double-decker rather than a coach on a prestige service, even by contemporary standards. In 1931 all passed to a London dealer, who had no difficulty in finding good homes for them on stage-carriage work all over the country. *The Omnibus Society*

3. Coming of Age

(North Western Road Car Co. Ltd. Official Time Table cover — March 30th, 1931 — Price 2D)

From 1930 North Western's well-laid foundations enabled it to consolidate its position through a dominant presence, infilling its chosen territory by steadily mopping up most of the remaining small operators. In the course of the decade roundly 30 would be acquired outright, and half as many again surrender routes whilst continuing to run marginal services, tours and excursions.

Additional links with Manchester for through services to Warrington, Northwich, and Knutsford had also been started in February 1930, in a new agreement with the Corporation to co-operate in the Altrincham area. This arose from the determination of Manchester's new General Manager, Stuart Pilcher, to forestall the imminent electrification of the Manchester–Altrincham commuter railway (commissioned in May 1931) and also potentially restrictive interpretations of the 1930 Road Traffic Act, by converting to local and limited-stop bus operation the tram services from the city, for which North Western would be a useful ally. Within the company's own sphere, many journeys on the Stockport–Altrincham services were projected through to Warrington, Stockport–Macclesfield buses to Leek, and Macclesfield–Altrincham buses to Lymm.

The 1930 Act reinforced the company's position as a major regional operator, but it was not all plain sailing. Cheshire County Council objected to 83 of North Western's applications, the two railway companies to 20, and even Manchester Corporation could not resist a 'dig' here and there. Most of Cheshire's objections were to test the water and establish the County's right to put its views to the Traffic Commissioners, for this was a new game for everybody. One can imagine the consternation at Charles Street when it was revealed that Stockport intended to apply to run out as far as Buxton and Hayfield, such was the Corporation's strength of feeling over the tramway-competition issue.

It had been nursing yet another grievance ever since the 1928 extension of the Buxton and Hayfield services into Manchester, even with protective fares for its tramways. Following lease expiry and boundary changes the Manchester line was now owned by Stockport as far as the municipal boundary at Lloyd Road, Levenshulme, joint tram services to the city centre having started on 1 February 1924.

George Cardwell, elevated from NWRCC General Manager to Managing Director in 1930 and also to the Tilling/BAT Board, also discovered at the eleventh hour that the Corporation was applying for Road Service Licences 'all over the borough'. When challenged

The Brush body on Tilling-Stevens B10A2 No 451 of 1930 looked a little more up-to-date than its predecessors. It is accompanied on excursion or rail-replacement duties by a contemporary Dennis EV with Strachans bodywork (RB 1580), used for a couple of years after acquisition in 1933 with the business of Hands Garage of Matlock. This bus was not rebodied and would be sold off in 1938. *Ian Allan Library*

it admitted its plans would cause a conflict of interests, yet affirmed its wish to 'remain on friendly terms'. Nobody was sure of the Commissioners' likely stance on the licensing of company and municipal services in urban areas, but as the Commissioner-elect for the North Western Traffic Area, Sir William Chamberlain, had been a municipal manager at Oldham, Leeds and Belfast, Stockport felt it was 'on a good wicket'. Unwilling to jeopardise highly remunerative services and wanting to stabilise its position in the town, North Western decided to pay to Stockport all its net receipts on parallel services within the borough, as well as continuing to charge protective fares over tram routes.
A legal document to this effect, also confirming Stockport's withdrawal of its Buxton and Hayfield applications, was signed on 14 January 1931, just before the Commissioners' initial hearings commenced.

In the event, a pragmatic view favoured established operators regardless of ownership. On the final stretch into Manchester similar provisions had, of course, been in force since 1928. In consequence, for the rest of the decade there was an interesting reversal of the usual state of affairs, in that North Western's board referred to Stockport Corporation as 'the pirate', with little right to get involved in bus operations at all, whilst conceding that it was justified in protecting its tramway investment. Warrington also reappeared on the agenda at this crucial time, as the Traffic Commissioners amended that agreement to prevent company buses from carrying any local passengers between the town centre and 440 yards beyond the tram termini at Stockton Heath or Latchford, except on Sunday mornings before the trams started. A 'silver lining' saw compensatory payments cease. Overall, the directors were greatly relieved when 122 licence applications of 124 lodged were granted without modification!

In 1931 the operational headquarters moved into a new building on the opposite side of Charles Street, the former offices becoming a staff social club and canteen. Amongst all the changes the company was still infilling its territory, one instance being a Winsford–Cuddington service usefully extended to Warrington in December 1931, another an equally speculative extension of a Warrington–Knutsford service northwards to Wigan and southwards to Lower Peover, a small community south of Knutsford which could never have been a serious traffic objective! Joint operation with LUT commenced early in 1932, usually amounting to six round-trips per day until November 1939. It was a remarkable sally into each other's sphere of operations, with no commonality of patronage and only the

dubious merit of penetrating each other's territory to the same extent; this may have been the rationale for stopping it short at Lower Peover, rather than just a few miles further on, at Middlewich. Surprisingly, although the northern stretch was to remain on NWRCC maps until 1959, for the previous 20 years it had operated over just the Cheshire section, worked solely by North Western, never to regain daily operation.

In the years 1932-4 there was a determined effort to mop up competition in the Peak District, particularly around Matlock, where the company already had a foothold, having replaced the District Council's cable tramway service up Matlock Bank in 1927. This hill was so steep that buses had to zig-zag across it on side streets when climbing; a ½d surcharge was applied to all fares and paid over to the Council to help extinguish its capital debt, and there was a 1d differential between the fares up and down. A local garage inherited in 1933 through an acquisition was significantly enlarged later.

Around Manchester, further joint operations were often replacements for services run by the few remaining small operators, including Heald Green/Styal (ex Organ & Wachter in 1933), Hale Barns via Altrincham (ex Sykes, 1933), and Woodford (ex Sharp's, 1936). By no means were these smaller operators 'men of straw'; Sharp's of Longsight had been able to afford an *avant garde* AEC 'Q' saloon for its service between Woodford and Winton, which it sensibly retained for its ongoing tours and excursions. Goodfellow Services of Hyde latterly operated from Manchester to Bolton, Bramhall, and Alderley as well as locally, and some of the 10 Thornycrofts passed to North Western in 1933 were used for two years before sale to SHMD, whilst Gilfords acquired from T. Slack & Sons of Darley Dale ran for three more years after a 1934 takeover.

The year 1933 saw express-service expansion come once again to the fore, often in concert with fellow BET/TBAT companies such as Ribble and BMMO ('Midland Red'). North Western thereby became a more significant player between Manchester and London and a leading participant in the Tyne–Tees–Mersey

No apology is offered for using this historic 'still' from an amateur ciné film taken outside Woodford Aerodrome (part of A. V. Roe's manufacturing complex) on 23 June 1934, when Sir Alan Cobham's Flying Circus gave an Air Display. The bus, North Western 194 (LG 3621), is an ex-Goodfellow/Hyde Thornycroft BCs of 1930, operating a duplicate working and displaying 'Bramhall/ Southfield House'. Acquired in 1933, it would be sold two years later to SHMD, which immediately had it rebodied. *North West Film Archive at Manchester Metropolitan University*

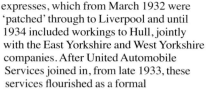

THE above is a reproduction of the type of Coach generally used on the Limited Stop Express Services operated by the Company:

To LONDON
LOWESTOFT
NEWCASTLE-UPON-TYNE
SCARBOROUGH
BRIDLINGTON
LIVERPOOL
LLANDUDNO
Etc.

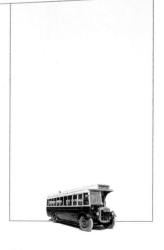

expresses, which from March 1932 were 'patched' through to Liverpool and until 1934 included workings to Hull, jointly with the East Yorkshire and West Yorkshire companies. After United Automobile Services joined in, from late 1933, these services flourished as a formal 'Tyne–Tees–Mersey Pool', in spite of considerable competition from some long-established independents. After some were acquired, and conflicting conditions in three Traffic Areas traversed had been resolved, the Pool settled down, North Western having the greatest mileage-entitlement, at 25%, and services via Bradford and to Middlesbrough, a summer extension from the latter to Redcar being added subsequently.

North Western also shared, with Eastern Counties, a Liverpool–Manchester–Lowestoft service pioneered by a Liverpool independent recently acquired by Ribble. Another takeover resulted in Charles Street's managing, for just over 20 years, a subsidiary with separately identified coaches, namely Majestic Express Motors Ltd, of London, which company's Manchester–London night service was acquired jointly with Midland Red in June 1933 but which thereafter was administered from Stockport. Fingland's Hire Cars Ltd of Manchester had been a pioneer on the service and preferred to operate jointly until selling its share in 1936, which explains why one daily trip in each direction started or finished at Fingland's garage in Wilmslow Road, Rusholme — a situation that was to continue until the 1960s.

Friction with Warrington Corporation re-emerged in 1935 when the terminus for the buses replacing its final tram service to Latchford was cut back 100 yards, and North Western sought to move its 'boundary' further in. There followed a 'tit-for-tat' battle of proposals, objections and counter-proposals, during which Warrington failed in its duty to notify the Traffic Commissioners that North Western would be affected by an encroaching extension from Stockton Heath along Chester Road towards the 'Dog & Dart'. After the acrimony died down there was a genuine attempt to arrive at a basis for joint working to Stretton and Thelwall, to which points the company was by then working regular 'shorts' as well as a new local service to Lymm Church,

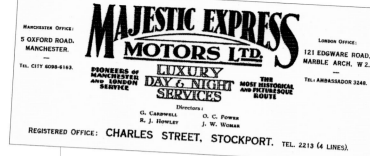

under the 1931 limitations, but this too foundered amid disagreements over the division of receipts and mileage.

Although Manchester had numbered all bus routes in the city in March 1930, including those run 'By Arrangement', North Western resolutely clung to its own series for several more years, both internally and in public timetables, though mercifully these numbers were not displayed on the buses. In January 1936 the company did renumber almost all its services, generally bringing them into line with those of most other operators on joint services, the changes being so drastic that only three of 162 retained their former numbers. To display them, twin-track number blinds were fitted to dash panels or nearside bulkheads of all buses. Rear route information on saloons had since the start of the decade been confined to a three-line slip-board at waistrail level, but by 1938 a single-line destination blind above the rear window was being specified.

The appointment in 1936 of North Western's Chief Engineer, C. W. Wroth, as General Manager of Stockport Corporation Transport came as quite a surprise after 12 years' service. His final responsibilities had included 700 drivers, 180 mechanics and 80 cleaners, while his period in office had witnessed fleet expansion from 92 to 500 vehicles, latterly running 18 million miles per annum. He was succeeded by W. S. Quinsey, of sister BET company Yorkshire Woollen District Transport. Wroth's move should have improved the relationship with Stockport, but instead this was soured when, without consultation, the Corporation introduced double-deckers on co-ordinated services to Adswood and then, in January 1937, applied for a new cross-town service from Offerton to Heaton Moor (Green End). North Western felt it should share in that, as the outer end adjoined its assumed territory, and the real objective was Manchester via Burnage. The issue was deemed so crucial that

Cardwell, as Chairman, attended Traffic Court to contend that the Corporation had since 1927 superimposed excessive bus services over the company's routes, after expressing a need only to protect its tramways. On this occasion the Corporation won, and the company decided on damage-limitation by suggesting a joint traffic pool over a wide area. Both general managers were deputed to negotiate detail, but municipal harness apparently had not suited Wroth; he had resigned in November 1937 and moved on to an overseas post back in the BET fold, finally to distinguish his career as General Manager of PMT from 1942 to 1958. At Stockport he was succeeded in May 1938 by E. B. Baxter from Bradford, following which, in August 1939, both parties approved the scheme, but this was stillborn, as World War 2 intervened.

The Congleton and Biddulph districts were in the spotlight from 1935 to 1939, much to the chagrin of PMT, which, as Potteries Electric Traction from 1898 to 1933, had been successor to the North Staffordshire [steam] Tramways Co, taken over as BET's very first tramway subsidiary, in 1896. A stand-off was sparked

by North Western's proposed acquisition in 1936/7 of Biddulph & District Motor Services and Sutton's Bus Co of Knypersley, with basic garaging, resolved only by the sale of some B&D buses and Sutton's routes to PMT. The railway companies had taken no financial interest in PMT because of its genesis as a statutory tramway undertaking, a lack of profit and continuing acrimony through much of the 1920s with the municipalities it served. The 'Biddulph question' was to remain a sore point, aggravated by some surreptitious infilling on local services by PMT during World War 2, and in the interim Biddulph was reluctantly accepted by both parties as a 'common town'.

In the final year of peace North Western fortuitously acquired the businesses of almost all remaining stage-carriage operators in its rural territory, namely Bostock's of Congleton, Broadhead of Bollington, Thompson of Northwich and Firth & Kirkpatrick of Marple; Hulley's of Baslow and nearby Silver Service of Darley Dale were among the very few to escape the Road Car's clutches.

The 1930s also proved to be 'glory days' inasmuch as the fleet was transformed by heavy investment in new rolling-stock, as well as judicious rebodying on a largescale. Even some new and recently delivered vehicles were rebodied, in order to secure the best possible combination of engines, chassis and body. The petrol-electrics had made their last journeys at Easter 1930, but inherited acquisitions in the new decade increased variety, militating against the standardisation so assiduously achieved.

At the start of the decade virtually the whole fleet had represented mid-1920s styling, buses and coaches alike having high chassis frames, tumble-home side panels, 'matchstick' window pillars, canvas-covered matchboarded roofs and generally uncompromising appearance, including in most respects the bodies on 25 Leyland Tiger 'coaches' recently bought primarily for the London service. Deliveries of four-cylinder petrol-engined Tilling-Stevens B10s would continue until late 1932, by which time General Manager Walter Womar was on the defensive in insisting that such vehicles were quite adequate for bus work. Likewise the Tigers' bodies had certainly

not represented contemporary coach design, being obsolete before they took to the road, with limited interior luggage space (by the rear entrance) as well as a roof-rack. They also featured an offside rear wheelarch seat at 45° to the direction of travel, which must have seemed of dubious merit to the passengers affected. Sold off in 1931, they would last years longer elsewhere as acceptable stage-carriage buses. Given the Tiger's reputation for reliability and speed and a pressing need to obtain vehicles for the London service, the board must have sanctioned their purchase as a stopgap solution.

As early as May 1931 no fewer than 184 vehicles (50% of the fleet) had been fitted with interior heating, all saloons were being fitted with more-informative front destination equipment neatly 'faired in' to the roof contour (replacing the previous styles perched on the front dome), and the 1930 Tilling-Stevens were receiving more-comfortable seating. The destination indicators installed over the queue barriers at Lower Mosley Street in October 1931 were possibly salvaged from those replaced on the buses at this time.

Technical aspects had developed apace, in bodywork and ancillary equipment as well as engines, and vehicle styling had altered dramatically. In 1931 there was a transition from base metal to pure gold, when 12 Leyland Tiger TS1s with up-to-date Harrington coachwork arrived for long-distance work, to be

Tilling-Stevens 558, a 1931 Brush-bodied 35-seater, takes a rest at Buxton in the late 1930s. It would be withdrawn and sold to a Leeds dealer in 1939 yet managed to reappear in Stockport during the war, with the Civil Defence organisation. *Mervyn Robertson / Online Transport Archive*

Harrington and Eastern Counties bodies on the 1931/2 Leyland Tigers represented a step-change from the contemporary Tilling-Stevens in terms of appearance and comfort. Even so, No 585 of 1932, seen here in Llandudno, was updated only three years later with new half-canopy Harrington coachwork. Unfortunately it was requisitioned in 1941, never to return. *Senior Transport Archive*

followed in 1932 by 25 similar Eastern Counties products on TS4 chassis. The arrival in 1932 of J. F. (later Sir Frederick) Heaton as Tilling Group Chairman led to changes in bus purchasing, the connection with Tilling-Stevens being replaced by a mandatory policy in favour of Bristol chassis produced in-house by the Bristol Tramways & Carriage Co. However, not only was Bristol's output insufficient for Group requirements at that time, but only heavyweight chassis were being produced. North Western had found its Leyland Tigers of 1931/2 to be good workhorses but in the interim switched to lighter-weight Dennis Lancet chassis as closer equivalents to the Tilling-Stevens for stage-carriage work, a demonstrator having proved satisfactory on the Buxton route in July 1932; by 1938 another 63 had been ordered. Although six normal-control Leyland Cubs had arrived at Easter 1933 as 20-seaters for narrow roads in the Peak District, these were augmented in 1934 by six sleeker Dennis Aces, of which two intended primarily for private hires had Harrington (instead of ECOC) bodies. The Lancets purchased for bus work in 1934/5 arrived firstly with full-canopy bodies and then in half-canopy versions (see below), all with four-cylinder petrol engines and ungainly protruding radiators which implied more power than they possessed, and were derived from an Armstrong-Saurer design which Dennis had gained rights to manufacture. Although they were an improvement on the Tilling-Stevens, their relative

◄ Drivers of this *avant-garde* 'mean machine' must have felt very superior amidst the hordes of Tilling-Stevens, in its early days. No 206 was the 1932 Dennis-bodied Lancet demonstrator which convinced the company to standardise on the marque for bus work until Bristols became more readily available. Seen here at Buxton's Market Place terminus in May 1937, it would be discarded just two years later. *Mervyn Robertson / Online Transport Archive*

In 1934 the prewar full-canopy body reached its final stage of development, and later would change only in detail behind the front bulkhead for half-canopy ► buses. Luxury seating and curtained windows had already been specified for the Eastern Counties bodywork on this Mk I Dennis Lancet, 622 (JA 2222), one of 30 which all gave 12 years' service; this example not only helped out at LPTB's Addlestone garage during 1940/1 but after disposal crossed the Channel to help with United Nations refugee relief work. *The Omnibus Society*

Two more gems at Buxton in the 1937 Coronation period: 1934 ► Dennis Lancet 643, with a standard ECOC body, on the 73 to Bakewell via Monyash, and, alongside, ECW-rebodied Tilling-Stevens B10A2 528, returning to its Congleton base on one of the six weekly journeys of the 41 via Allgreave. The Dennis spent time with LPTB in 1940/1 and was withdrawn in 1946, but the 1931 Tilling served for a further two years. *Mervyn Robertson / Online Transport Archive*

Taking pride of place in this August 1936 view near Lower Mosley Street is rebodied 1929 Tilling-Stevens No 384, awaiting redeployment along with 1934 Dennis Lancet 638. Both vehicles had been fitted with route-number indicators, the Dennis unusually so on the nearside bulkhead. Both would be withdrawn 10 years later.
The Omnibus Society's Lawton Collection

A year after the Leyland Cubs arrived six Dennis Aces were purchased to augment them and represented a significant improvement in appearance. Four, including 651 (JA 2251), were bodied by Eastern Counties, but the final pair had even sleeker Harrington bodywork. All six would remain in service until 1945.
Roy Marshall collection

Leyland Tiger TS6 No 661 (JA 2261) of 1934, seen in Hyde Market Place in August 1936, was amongst the first coaches with the Harrington half-canopy coachwork. These ran with sealed carburettors in their first six months and allegedly were very fast. Ironically 661 was to receive a utility Burlingham bus body in 1943, in which form it would be exchanged in 1946 for an East Midland prewar Bristol.
The Omnibus Society's Lawton Collection

lack of power ensured that most were later banished to the flatter territory around Northwich. Neater radiators on subsequent batches of Lancet IIs harmonised much better with the new half-canopy body, a trio delivered in 1936 with Gardner 5LW engines being supplemented in July 1938 by another three fitted with Dennis Lanova four-cylinder diesels.

For coaching work Leyland's Tiger chassis was preferred, and subsequent prewar deliveries set new standards with Harrington coachwork of half-canopy style. The first appeared in September 1934, attracting Ribble deputations to Charles Street led by Major Hickmott (MD) and Captain Betteridge (Chief Engineer), doubtless at the instigation of W. S. Wreathall, who was Chairman of Ribble and still on North Western's board. From this one might assume that Ribble's distinctive half-canopy buses and coaches of the 1935-40 period were inspired by North Western's initial front-end design, being very different in style from Ribble's pre-1935 intake. A small batch of forward-control Cubs appeared in 1936 as 24-seat Harrington coaches of similar appearance, and a final six the following year as stylish 25-seat buses.

One of the Leyland Tiger TS8/
Harrington coaches of 1937 when new,
in a livery of off-white with red relief,
at speed somewhere in the West
Midlands while on the London service.
*Mervyn Robertson / Online Transport
Archive*

A scaled-down, 24-seat version of the
Harrington coach body was applied to
six Leyland Cubs in 1936, which must
have taxed their performance somewhat,
yet they remained on strength until 1950.
No 723 is at the parking ground behind
Mersey Square bus station on stage-
carriage relief duty, typically displaying
'DUPLICATE' via 'DUPLICATE'. *J. W. Hillmer*

A final variant on the Leyland Cub theme occurred in 1937 with
the arrival of six hybrids of the new half-canopy coach and bus
designs. These Harrington 25-seaters were also withdrawn in
1950, having latterly been nicknamed 'Flying Fleas' by some of
their regular passengers on works services. The fleet number of
JA 7783, seen here on Salford dealer Frank Cowley's premises
after disposal, had been 883. *Senior Transport Archive*

The half-canopy ECW body improved the looks of Mk I Dennis Lancets, but belying their impressive appearance was a relative lack of torque from their four-cylinder engines. Seen ex-works in 1935, with route boards for the Manchester–Greenfield service, No 694 commendably served for 14 years. *Roy Marshall collection*

Amongst the first new buses to have the half-canopy ECOC body was Lancet 702 of 1935. It would also operate for LPTB in 1940/1 and thereafter serve the company until 1949. Here it is at Buxton, short-working to Chapel-en-le-Frith on the Glossop service, in prewar days. Exceptionally, the destination and intermediate displays have been transposed for this departure. *Mervyn Robertson / Online Transport Archive*

The 1936 Lancet IIs looked much less aggressive than did their immediate predecessors, their appearance marred only by their offset radiators. Not long before its demise in 1952 No 752 — one of a trio equipped with the preferred Gardner 5LW engine — was photographed duplicating the 31 service from the still-cobbled Parker Street city terminus. *Senior Transport Archive*

Once Bristol output could meet Tilling Group demand, Gardner 5LW-engined J- and then L-type chassis became mandatory for bus work. In nearly all these cases Eastern Counties ('Eastern Coach Works' from 1936) supplied the bodywork, to a design that had matured from the solid yet up-to-date full-canopy style of 1932 into a half-canopy layout akin to the contemporary Harrington coaches. Internally they all offered a high standard of passenger comfort, with high-backed coach seats, decorative light fittings mounted on the window pillars, draw-back curtains to each saloon window and decorated ceiling panels. Ironically the new bus design had first been used to rebody many of the post-1927 Tilling-Stevens, but retention of their archaic-looking radiators and low bonnet-lines produced an incongruous top-heavy appearance. Indeed, this truly reflected that they were overburdened with their new bodies, a situation highlighted by their high-pitched sound under stress and a diminutive four-cylinder engine, displayed whenever drivers had to leave the bonnet-side open in hot weather! Their unique characteristic was a loud tinkling sound caused by vibration of a loose-fitting brass sleeve over the permanently attached starter-handle if, typically, the latter was not secured by its retaining strap. As late as August 1938 Tilling-Stevens were still allocated to every garage except Urmston. The ECW half-canopy body was also used in 1938 on a dozen Tiger TS7 chassis, delivered new in 1935 as Harrington coaches, which before entering traffic had exchanged their bodies for those of 1931-built Harrington saloons. Lest it be thought that management had lost touch with reality, this was justified by placing the newest coach bodies on the smoothest-running petrol-engined chassis!

Technical progress was not always a straight-line trend, and new developments sometimes had unforeseen side-effects on previously adequate components. The post-1928 Tilling-Stevens had front-wheel stub-axles replaced by the manufacturer at half cost, following some hair-raising wheel-shedding incidents, including one through an Oldham house window in November 1932, ex bus 432. Even the first Leyland Tigers needed their

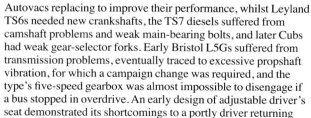

Bristol JO5G 789 looks a potent force on its way to Hayfield in June 1938 as it waits for traffic lights at the Grosvenor Street/Brook Street junction in Manchester. Alongside are an early-1930s Austin car and a Manchester tram on the 35B, routed through to Hazel Grove, which would trail the bus as far as Stockport. Two MCTD inspectors with shining shoes stand on the corner to ensure that tram and bus drivers comply with a major one-way traffic scheme, so recently introduced that inbound tracks and overhead are still connected. *Greater Manchester Transport Society*

Autovacs replacing to improve their performance, whilst Leyland TS6s needed new crankshafts, the TS7 diesels suffered from camshaft problems and weak main-bearing bolts, and later Cubs had weak gear-selector forks. Early Bristol L5Gs suffered from transmission problems, eventually traced to excessive propshaft vibration, for which a campaign change was required, and the type's five-speed gearbox was almost impossible to disengage if a bus stopped in overdrive. An early design of adjustable driver's seat demonstrated its shortcomings to a portly driver returning from Middlewich, when he tried to change its position while on the move. The mechanism collapsed as he was speeding along the Byley straight, and, peering through the very bottom of the windscreen, with hands higher than his shoulders, he eventually regained control by shuffling his back upwards against the bulkhead behind him. As the bulkhead window shattered from the undue pressure, he was lucky that neither he nor any of his passengers were injured by splintered glass, and fortunately the bus was halted without further incident.

A B10A model of 1929,
No 339 received its half-cab
Eastern Counties body in 1935
and served until 1946.
Here it is, just before the war,
on the A6 at the Whaley Bridge
terminus of the hilly 47 route,
offering a connection with
No 792 on the 27 in the
background (see page 31).
In the foreground is the
predecessor to the 'zebra
crossing', a double row of
studs across the road flanked
on each side by an unlit
yellow globe on a striped post,
known as a 'Belisha Beacon',
after Leslie Hore-Belisha,
the Minister of Transport
who had introduced them
(as well as the Highway Code)
in 1934. *Mervyn Robertson /
Online Transport Archive*

On the other hand, vehicle reliability had improved so much that even by 1932 it had been possible to extend servicing to 10,000-mile intervals, at which an eight-hour 'light docking' was carried out at garages. Every 30,000 miles buses were sent to Stockport for a 'medium heavy dock', effectively a light overhaul without wholesale removal of larger mechanical units or a body-lift, although engines, clutches, gearboxes and fuel and ignition systems were subjected to close inspection, cleaning, machining and recalibration or replacement, as necessary. Complete overhauls, scheduled at 60,000-mile intervals, took a working week, of which three days were allocated to a thorough repainting. About 11 buses a week received this treatment, in addition to others receiving only a repaint. A unit-replacement system was no longer standard practice, making it possible to reduce stocks of major items to minimal levels to cover only accident repairs and serious breakdowns. The docking bays were backed up by well-equipped specialist workshops, all inter-connected by overhead runway hoists. During the decade there had been a battle between petrol and diesel fuel, not helped by arbitrary political decisions on the taxation of these alternatives. Between 1933 and 1938 fuel costs rose on average by 30% — and markedly more so on diesel, as soon as it gained the ascendancy, the 1935 Budget having wrought particular havoc.

The Manchester joint services were still single-deck-operated until the late 1930s, just six lowbridge Leyland TD1 Titans having replaced the Tilling-Stevens open-toppers in 1931. Why they had been ordered is debatable, the planned limited-stop services along the Altrincham corridor seemingly the most likely candidates. However, the latter were vetoed by the Traffic Commissioners, probably at railway instigation, and, just to add a further twist, the licences issued for the Manchester–Halebarns service, then joint with MCTD and Sykes of Hale, specifically

NORTH WESTERN ROAD CAR CO. LTD

IN ASSOCIATION WITH L.M.S. AND L.N.E. RAILWAYS

OFFICIAL TIME TABLE

January 1st, 1936   PRICE **2**ᴰ

▲ One of the six all-Leyland Titan TD1s which sufficed for North Western's double-deck requirements until 1938, at the Glossop terminus of the 6 and 125, in company with a contemporary Tilling-Stevens (516: DB 9416), both equipped to display the new 1936 route numbers. Whilst the Leyland was sold in 1938 and passed to Crosville in 1949, the Tilling received a 1935 half-canopy ECOC body in 1939 from an earlier counterpart, extending its NWRCC career until 1948.
J. F. Higham / The Omnibus Society

The Bristol Ks of 1938/9 were attractive and comfortable vehicles for their time and, unlike most of their successors, lacked the upper-deck front-window ventilators which impeded forward vision for passengers. Here 953 loads in Altrincham bus station on local service 181 to Riddings Road Estate, Timperley, shortly before rebodying in 1951.
J. W. Hillmer

One of the Harrington-bodied Tiger TS8s at Lower Mosley Street on a Tyne–Tees–Mersey duty, just before receiving new Windover coachwork in 1950 (and renumbering as 391), gaining it seven more years of service. The 1939 Bristol K5G (978) on the 28 was also on the verge of receiving a new body and, renumbered 458, would last until 1964. *J. W. Hillmer*

Tickets used on some MCTD joint services until *c*1954.

banned double-deckers in Hale. Accordingly all six Titans were delicensed for at least their first winter and apparently came to be used only for seasonal augmentation and special events. In such a guise they were employed in August 1936 to deal with heavy loadings to the Mottram Show, which thereafter saw them put to regular use on the 125 from Hyde via Mottram to Glossop (then joint only with SHMD). That possibly prompted the company to apply to run double-deckers on the busy Manchester–Buxton service, refused by the Traffic Commissioners in 1937. Later that year Oldham Corporation asked North Western to match its application to operate double-deckers on the 2 from Manchester to Shaw and Newhey, and thus the Titans at last saw full utilisation in their final year of service, being based at Glossop, Oldham, Manchester (summer) and Stockport (winter). All were withdrawn after the 1938 summer season and promptly sold to the Bristol Tramways & Carriage Co.

The Titans were displaced by the delivery of the first orders for Bristol K5Gs with ECW bodywork, which vehicles could initially be used only at Manchester and Urmston. These had almost the same high standards of passenger comfort as the contemporary saloons, excepting their lowbridge upper-deck layout and the lack of curtains to the windows. Although ordered in three batches they amounted to 64 double-deckers in barely two years. This massive increment led to problems in their deployment, as the Traffic Commissioners refused their use on no fewer than 54 services across rural Cheshire, in view of objections from the County and 12 local councils, on grounds of 'rural amenity', and also from the two railway companies in respect of particular services. Thus the new double-deckers were initially under-utilised, other than on routes from Manchester to Flixton, Newhey and Hayfield (which did gain approval) and from Glossop to Hyde and to Chorlton. They would, however, be a blessing in disguise.

A view across the docking bays at Charles Street, possibly taken just postwar but revealing only prewar rolling-stock. From left to right they are a 1931 Tiger TS1/Harrington (1934 rebody), a 1937 Cub/Harrington, a 1936 Dennis Lancet II/ECW, a 1938/9 Bristol K5G/ECW, a 1938 Dennis Lancet II/ECW and two Tigers with late-prewar Harrington coachwork. *Senior Transport Archive*

Some of the 1932 Tigers survived well into postwar days with their 1936 coachwork, and this one, still looking quite presentable, is taking a breather on the overflow area at Lower Mosley Street on 8 September 1951 in its final weeks of service. In the background is a mural (shortly to be renovated) listing many of the wayside stops in all directions on express services operated from Manchester. *R. L. Wilson / Online Transport Archive*

5. Testing the Mettle

Through sound management the company entered the war in good shape on 3 September 1939. The fleet had been substantially modernised, and standardisation had recovered somewhat, if less prevalent than a decade earlier. A large contingent of double-deckers was entering service, ready to cope with the huge increase in passengers on cessation of private motoring due to stringent fuel rationing. Fortunately the mileage run by diesel-engined buses had recently eclipsed that of the petrols, having just reached 68% of the total, average consumption across the fleet being 13.5mpg for diesels against only 7.4mpg for petrol engines. The garages and bus stations were in good order, most having been recently modernised or extended; a garage extension was in progress at Altrincham, and a combined facility at Macclesfield was so new that only the garage had been opened by May 1939, the office and passenger areas not being completed until December.

Complying with Civil Defence advice, provision of air-raid shelters at garages and bus stations had been started in 1938. At Charles Street work was still outstanding, so trenches protected by sandbags had to suffice initially. Office-window blackout was economically obtained using old indicator blinds painted black overall and trimmed to size. Garage and workshop rooflights were given a coat of blue paint, and light bulbs dipped in orange paint. These measures were so effective that workshop staff soon complained of severe headaches brought on by poor illumination even in daytime, and they had to be moderated to restore output. At Macclesfield, Matlock and Glossop garage roofs were conspicuous from the air and were painted in camouflage patterns, fortunately not necessary elsewhere. North Western's buses were quickly given dark roofs, the General Manager informing the board that some 467 had been painted battleship grey in the single month of September 1939. However, the emergency measures had such an impact that by December 26% of the fleet was overdue the 60,000-mile heavy-docking procedure, a situation worsened by an immediate 15% loss of fitters to the Armed Forces as reservists and volunteers, as well as by temptations of better pay elsewhere.

On 17 September emergency timetables and crew rosters were introduced which reduced fleet mileage by a third. This was achieved by reducing daytime frequencies and minimising journeys during darkness, although lengthening nights made it impossible to eliminate the latter, as the evening rush-hour extended almost to 7pm, and most factory staff were soon working prodigious amounts of overtime. Some stage-carriage services were withdrawn altogether, yet very few stretches of route were left totally uncovered. On the other hand, all express services were cancelled outright from 18 September, except for the Tyne–Tees–Mersey, Blackpool and Barnsley services, which would soon be affected, as well as that to Bradford via Halifax, which continued to run throughout the war, Sundays excepted, presumably because it afforded intermediate connections not achievable by rail. The last request of the Railways Joint Committee, before suspension 'for the duration', was for connections at stations to be checked during timetable revisions, because of significant alterations to railway services.

Although fleet strength had reached 586 by 31 August 1939, having briefly peaked at 603, the fuel allocation was thought sufficient for only 300 buses. It had been based on 50% of the 1938 usage, but as North Western's proportion of petrol- to diesel-powered vehicles had changed so much, a significant variation needed negotiating, 12,384 gallons of petrol and 12,965 gallons of diesel per week being amended to 6,269 gallons of petrol and 16,782 gallons of diesel. This was estimated to allow for 83% of diesel running (hitherto 68%), achieved by using diesels more intensively and minimising petrol mileage. The work carried out just before the war to increase diesel storage was fortunate in its timing. Where possible, it had been done by simply switching over disproportionate depot storage between the two fuels, although this entailed a laborious tank-cleaning process.

A further stratagem was reallocation of vehicle types to territories more suited to their characteristics (or inherent vices, as the drivers might have said), subject to any special needs.

TRAVELLING IN WARTIME IS **A DIFFICULT BUSINESS** Don't make it harder by making Unnecessary Journeys The MONEY SAVED can be invested in **WAR SAVINGS**

The Company's Noted Long Distance Express Services are Cancelled for the Duration.

Hence repeated requests to travel only when strictly necessary, and to spend your Holidays at Home.

We, like you, look forward to the Restoration of Travel Amenities.

Prepare for that time by working and **SAVING for VICTORY.**

INVEST IN WAR SAVINGS

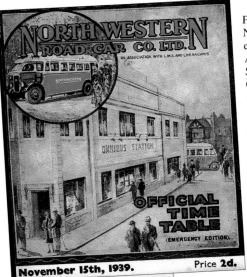

November 15th, 1939.   Price **2d.**

Petrol-engined Dennises ended up at Buxton, Northwich, Wilmslow and Stockport, diesel-engined examples being concentrated at Northwich, the few Aces at Buxton and Wilmslow, and the Tilling-Stevens restricted to Altrincham, Macclesfield, Oldham and Biddulph, whilst all the diesel Tigers were shared between Manchester and Stockport. Double-deck conversions continued as far as practicable to minimise duplication, Macclesfield, Northwich, and Wilmslow gaining K5G allocations in August, September and October 1939 respectively. The Traffic Commissioners had been replaced by wartime Regional Transport Commissioners with sweeping arbitrary powers, office-based rather than in open Traffic Court. As the publication of official *Notices & Proceedings* had been suspended, opposition was virtually silenced. All these efforts produced real dividends, for by November mileage for diesel buses reached 84%, and no lost mileage was attributed to lack of fuel, even though some new services had to be provided for those engaged in essential war work. The reduction in fleet mileage naturally affected revenue, which within a month fell by almost 14%, but there was even a beneficial side to this, as the income per car-mile rose from 9.07d to 12.08d with better utilisation of the licensed fleet.

The most practical way of conserving liquid fuel was to try gas propulsion, and North Western had instigated initial service trials in June 1939 with a French Gohin-Poulenc producer-gas unit. This was mounted within the rear panels of Bristol JO5G diesel-engined saloon 728, which in the following month completed more than 2,400 miles in service, with average anthracite consumption of 2lb (0.91kg) per mile. However, as the gas had a lower calorific value, power dropped to the extent that the differential unit had to be changed to maintain schedules. The only other serious problems were excessive cylinder wear and inadequate gas filters. For comparison purposes it was then decided to fit similar equipment, for which Bristol Tramways had acquired manufacturing rights, to 1932 Leyland Tiger TS4 No 602 (by then diesel-powered), but an initial promise of greater power was not fulfilled. To cap everything the Bristol later caught fire due to poor equipment ventilation but survived! In December 1939 a coke-fired producer-gas trailer was delivered to Charles Street, and petrol-engined Tiger 593 was slowly converted, albeit not tested for some months.

A second comprehensive emergency timetable had been imposed in November 1939, although fine-tuning continued as circumstances dictated. By December no fewer than 242 vehicles of the September fleet total of 594 had been delicensed, compared with a normal winter reduction of about 100. There was great concern for their safe long-term storage, as well as protection of the active fleet in the event of air raids. For the latter it was decreed that buses should be scattered around depot premises in groups of not more than 20, as far as practicable, wider dispersal being discounted due to the likelihood of frost damage and winter starting problems — a wise decision in view of what Mother Nature had up her sleeve! The situation was eventually alleviated by the requisitioning by the Armed Forces and various Government agencies of almost 50 buses and coaches, the conversion of eight as ambulances and the loan to London Transport in 1940, for up to nine months, of at least 16 Dennis Lancets, plus that of 17 Tilling-Stevens to Crosville for much longer periods. In addition 30 rebodied Tilling-Stevens were sold to the Bristol Tramways group.

There was a downside, however, as unexpected factors militated against fuel saving. Upon the immediate imposition of blackout regulations, drivers had been instructed not to exceed 10mph during hours of darkness, there being neither street lighting nor illumination from

Liverpool-bound on a Tyne–Tees–Mersey duty, 1938 Bristol L5G 915 braves out the elements stuck in a snowdrift on Standedge Summit in the bitter winter of 1940/1; hopefully its passengers and crew made it to the 'Floating Light' Inn or other refuge. It would serve the company until 1961 by dint of a new Burlingham body fitted in 1950. *Senior Transport Archive*

shop windows; much of the mileage was, in any case, run through countryside. Even headlights and sidelights were masked to the point of being merely 'markers'. Neither continuous slow running in low gear nor the excessive overloading which became commonplace were conducive to fuel economy. With most of the Tilling-Stevens relegated to rush-hour work and factory journeys even their fuel consumption increased, through being started from cold more than once a day! There was also an increase in fatal accidents during blackout hours, for which staff were mostly found blameless.

The Ministry of Defence could not decide on the most practical method of masking headlights, and although by October 1939 the active fleet had been modified twice there was further delay before this matter was finalised. There was a similar hiatus on interior lighting. In an attempt to 'square the circle' between sufficient diminution to meet regulations and adequate light for conductors to issue correct tickets and change, a deputation went to inspect a London Transport bus fitted with a practical and approved design of shield. Nevertheless, North Western had to get Home Office approval locally, a requirement which delayed fitment fleetwide until February 1940.

By the end of 1939 winter had truly set in, 12,640 miles being lost due to thick fogs in December. Much worse was to follow in the shape of heavy snowfalls well into the New Year, resulting in 171,600 lost miles in January and February, even though many buses were fitted with snow chains. Throughout January the temperature rose above freezing-point for only a few hours in total, and on the 20th of the month 6°F (–13°C) was experienced across the company's territory, causing many radiator failures in service. A major problem was an acute shortage of anti-freeze, the Government having commandeered all stocks of ethylene-glycol, its main constituent, for the Armed Forces. Almost the final straw was a blizzard on 26 January, so severe that some buses were snowbound on the road for several days; hardly anything ran for a day or two afterwards, and some services around Macclesfield and Buxton were suspended for four weeks. More heavy snow on 17 February saw sickness absence of platform staff peak at 26%, whilst frost damaged the heaters on 163 buses before the thaw.

In the spring of 1940 application was made to renew a number of seasonal express licences, the 'Phoney War' period prior to May 1940 having not seen the immediate *Blitzkrieg* initially feared. But there were soon admonitions to avoid all non-essential travel, to preserve facilities for war workers and Forces

personnel! A few express services were reinstated, such as that from Manchester to North Wales at weekends (which ceased at the end of the 1941 season), and to Blackpool, but even the latter was withdrawn at short notice on 30 March 1942. By October 1941 a general shortage of buses had led to another Government-inspired campaign for the conversion of saloons to perimeter seating, thereby significantly increasing standing space, and North Western duly altered about 70 buses.

Warrington came to the fore briefly again in February 1942, attracting severe criticism from the local Trades Council over the lack of co-ordination between the Corporation's services and those of North Western, Crosville and Lancashire United, which meant that essential workers were often left behind at stops which partially filled company buses were prevented from serving. The companies offered to pick up on inward journeys only, paying 25% of this extra revenue to the Corporation (and variations thereon), but the latter stonewalled, paying lip-service to the need for co-ordination but not agreeing to any practical scheme. At a meeting at LUT's Atherton HQ the companies

▲ Perimeter seating being tried out by directors and Head Office staff posing as passengers on one of the well-appointed post-1935 ECW-bodied saloons. Note the segmented mirror on the bulkhead, emergency lighting shields and comfortable seats, although the unshrouded lamps would almost certainly have been disconnected 'for the duration'. The bowler-hatted gent in the light suit looks like J. W. Womar. *Greater Manchester Transport Society*

The Roe-bodied lowbridge utility Guy Arabs were amongst the better examples of their kind. Here No 26 of 1944 is completing a 'rounder' on the New Mills service, out via Marple and back via Disley, confusingly numbered the same in both directions. These buses gained route-number blinds not long before they received new Willowbrook bodies (in 1950), but perhaps this conductor has forgotten his bus has one, as they had to be changed from the upper deck. *Senior Transport Archive*

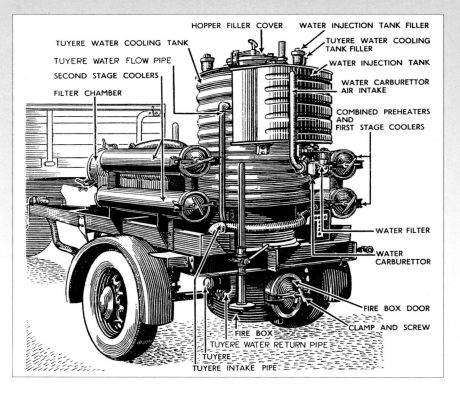

▲ This sketch from an instruction manual shows the general appearance of the producer-gas trailers that were forced on operators in the 1942-4 period. It is shown attached to a lorry, the Government's original intention being that they should be used for goods vehicles rather than buses. *The Omnibus Society*

agreed that progress was impossible in the face of such intransigence and that each should submit separate proposals at a later date.

During 1942 came six new Guy Arabs with utility lowbridge bodies — a welcome shot in the arm and the advance guard of 21 more to trickle through over the next three years, alongside three Daimlers. Whilst the chassis types were new to the fleet, fortunately all had Gardner engines. Welcome though they were, they represented a drop in the ocean relative to the number needed to keep the fleet up to date.

The most significant event of 1942, however, was the break-up in August of the Tilling-BAT group, due to a divergence of management philosophies, which must have been profound to have occurred in the darkest days of the war. Most companies remained with their existing management group, but the majority share-holding in North Western passed to BET, and that in Crosville in the opposite direction, to Tilling, which would have long-term implications for both companies, not least in terms of vehicle policy.

Having sold off the last unrebodied Tilling-Stevens in 1942, the company seized the opportunity to augment the active fleet the following year by rebodying 20 withdrawn TS4 and TS6 Tiger coaches as utility saloons, which the Blackpool firm of Burlingham had been authorised to build on forward-control chassis. All re-entered service in all-over grey, the older bodies being sold, the newer ones stored. North Western chose these rebodied Tigers to comply with a Ministry of War Transport directive of October 1942 requiring all operators of 150 buses or more to equip 10% of their fleets for producer-gas operation within nine months. The whole industry hated gas trailers because of their extra demand on limited maintenance facilities, as well as their unreliability and low efficiency, but perseverance was now demanded. North Western managed to convert only these additional buses before the programme was rescinded. The producer-gas Bristol was converted back to diesel in April/May 1944, although the last two Tiger conversions to gas were not completed until the following month. During that year a maximum of just under 2% of the company's mileage was operated by gas-fuelled vehicles, whereas diesels covered 80%, and petrols just 18%. Just three months later all the 'gas' buses were withdrawn for re-conversion with alacrity, after HMG unexpectedly announced that supplies of liquid fuel could at last be increased.

Off-peak frequencies were thereby modestly improved, providing better services for shoppers, in June 1944, by which time the company was employing a considerable number of conductresses to maintain services. Most were as reliable as their longer-serving male counterparts, many staying on after 1945, but unfortunately their record was tarnished by a minority who were regularly late for work and by a few who missed up to 50% of their duties.

Later in 1944 more authorised improvements were provided, mainly (due to staff shortages) as later evening journeys rather than better daytime frequencies, as had been intended. Towards the end of hostilities the war-weariness of some conductors showed in their not allowing the wartime union agreement of 12 standees on conventionally seated buses, leading to friction with equally war-weary passengers and management. Particularly high levels of absenteeism occurred early in 1945 during yet another spell of very bad weather, and, in a similar

Dennis Lancet 689 of 1935 became unique in 1943 when it was given an ECW 35-seat utility body sporting two route indicators, in contravention of Ministry of Supply specifications; as the chassis/body combination had remained unchanged, perhaps it was declared as an accident repair to circumvent them, because the equipment was available! Following withdrawal in 1951 it would be used as an office at Biddulph garage until commissioning of the joint NWRCC/PMT premises in 1960. *Senior Transport Archive*

▲ Dennis Lancet 706 (JA 5506) of 1935, seen on layover outside Buxton station in June 1945 whilst three American servicemen wait for something to happen. Bus roofs had been painted matt dark grey in 1939 but by this time had weathered to (or been repainted) a paler shade. *The Omnibus Society*

A 1945 scene at Northwich bus station, with 1939 Bristol Ks 963 and 962 loading for Winsford and Rudheath respectively. Both are in lined-out prewar livery with the addition of grey roofs and 'BRITISH BUSES' logos and legend on the upper deck sides. The latter were elements of a campaign to remind the public of the essential role buses had played during hostilities and thereby stave off the threat of nationalisation. *The Omnibus Society*

Macclesfield bus station and garage in Sunderland Street just after the war, with Guy/Roe utility 17 (BJA 136), without a route number blind, loading for route 24 to Gawsworth and Congleton. On the left is Bristol L5G/ECW 990 (AJA 190) on a town service to Forest Cottage, while ticking over in the background are three more Ls or JO5Gs. *Greater Manchester Transport Society*

vein, Macclesfield crews refused to work on VE Day (8 May) and VJ Day (15 August). By June 1945 staff shortage and absenteeism at Stockport, Manchester and Glossop was seriously affecting services and by November briefly peaked at 25% across the company. At Altrincham there was unrest over new schedules, and in Oldham reaction to unruly passengers (nothing is new!). Moderate relief was afforded by a rapid reduction in works services as many contracts for war materials were terminated at short notice. However, the era of many hours of near-compulsory overtime for platform staff had truly started.

Fortunately for the company's finances, private hires of less than 70 round-trip miles and excursions and tours of less than 50 miles were 'decontrolled' in June 1945 and just three months later were further relaxed on specified weekdays. As such duties were

among the attractions of working for the company, being beyond close supervision and the rigid discipline of the timetable, it was much preferred for overtime.

Commendably the company started to replace wooden-slatted seats on utilities with normal upholstery in March 1945, even before the final examples entered the fleet, and two months before the European war ended. Restoration of normal seating layouts in saloons also got underway, while deliveries of new buses to peacetime standards would resume early the following year. In readiness the Harrington coach bodies removed from the Leyland Tiger TS6s in 1943 were refurbished for remounting in 1946 on ten 1931 Tigers just returned in poor condition by the Ministry of Supply — a prelude to one of the most extensive sequences of rebodying ever carried out by a provincial operator.

6. Recovery

In mid-1946 a new General Manager took over the reins from
J. W. Womar, who had held the post since 1930, having joined the
company in its 'Peak District Committee' days, and now became
a BET executive director. Maintaining a remarkable degree of
continuity, he would return in 1948 for a further eight years as
Chairman. His successor was Tilling-trained H. G. R. Lambert,
General Manager of East Midland Motor Services, of
Chesterfield, also a one-time Tilling subsidiary that had been
reallocated to BET in 1942.

The company, like the nation, had won the war but had to win
the peace. Shortages of commonplace items continued, and many
basic materials remained on Government allocation, priority
being given to manufacturers engaged in export markets.
Particular concerns were that 225 buses (41% of the fleet) were
still petrol-driven, and there were only 94 double-deckers.
Nevertheless, by January 1945 less than 15% of mileage was
being run on petrol. Furthermore, although overall fleet condition
was generally better than average, many buses had been worked

so intensively, or for so long, that they were deemed beyond
redemption. In this category came the Dennis Aces, the Leyland
Lions and remaining 1933 Cubs and the acquired Dennises,
as well as an AEC Ranger. Their disposal was approved in
January 1945, as the last 10 Guy utilities were being delivered.
Even so, some worn-out vehicles had to remain in service, the
veteran Tilling-Stevens being prone to stalling on steep hills.
Male conductors usually helped by swinging the starting handle,
but if a conductress were aboard then the driver had no alternative,
before hastening back to the cab to drop the revs. Passengers
would then alight to walk to the summit, enabling the bus to
crawl up in first gear. Petrol-engined Dennises usually overcame
such obstacles, screaming in protest, but the Dennis O4 diesels
would emulate the Tilling-Stevens, and, with two or more steep
hills *en route* (as between Marple and Stockport), could
successively decant their passengers and end up way behind
schedule. One Stockport conductress gained the nickname
'Dirty Dolly', without any imputation as to her character,
because she could dive under the bonnet of an ailing bus and
often coax some power back with her ministrations, inevitably
ending up with very oily hands!

Other, more mechanically robust buses needed urgent
bodywork attention, and when Charles Street was over-stretched
recourse was made to outside contractors. One such was Bond's
of Wythenshawe, well-regarded for van and ambulance building
but diversifying into PSV work during the postwar 'scarcity
years', becoming one of the pioneer users of 'Claytonrite' rubber
window-glazing strip. It had a distinct advantage in having a sales
manager who, in a previous post with Brush Coachworks Ltd,
had established a good rapport with many operators' engineers.

Fortunately North Western must have lodged an early claim for
postwar requirements, as 92 Bristol L5G saloons were delivered
in 1946/7, notwithstanding the company's switch to the BET
group. New Brush bodies for the first 35 new L5Gs were in build
before Lambert's arrival, and also for 74 ten-year-old JO5Gs,
all resembling prewar styling, and their arrival enabled all the
full-canopied Dennis Lancets of 1934 to be sold off. These Brush
bodies had prewar-standard front indicators but none at the rear.

Well designed and comfortable by contemporary standards, like so many products of that era they would prove less durable than might have been expected. Their arrival enabled more weary Tilling-Stevens to be sold, some going to Midland Red's Stratford Blue subsidiary.

The bodywork on the other new Bristols was basically to ECW's standard postwar design. However, Lambert and his Chief Engineer, A. S. Woodgate (who had transferred from East Midland two years earlier), seemingly exerted influence on their detailed specification, as they had the single-blind front destination display used by East Midland since 1934, which became North Western's norm into the early 1950s. All the ECWs had above the rear window a single-line indicator, which remained unused before 1950, and their simplified front display must have saved on scarce supplies of linen during this period of strict austerity.

Just before Lambert's arrival, restoration of express services commenced in earnest, starting on 18 April 1946 with the two joint services from Manchester to Barnsley, followed on 3 June by the London service and, soon after, those to North Wales, Scarborough, Nottingham, and Blackpool. However, the Derby and Tyne–Tees–Mersey routes had to wait until the autumn before sufficient vehicles were available; very tight control had to be imposed over bookings because of strict duplication limits. At the same time the company was proclaiming its efforts to restore prewar service levels, although fares had scarcely altered since 1923. Given the degree of inflation caused by the war it was a major policy error, as the effects were masked for a while by continuing high levels of traffic and receipts per car-mile. Once petrol was taken off ration, fuel duty increased drastically in the 1950-2 period, other factors intervened, and above-inflation fares increases became essential (though not readily understood by passengers), helping to perpetuate a steady downward trend in patronage.

During 1946 negotiations with Warrington Corporation were at last fruitful, a 10-year agreement being reached that June to split both mileage and revenue on an equal basis on local services between alternating town termini, at Central and Bank Quay stations, and Stretton ('Cat & Lion') and Thelwall ('Pickering Arms'). Implemented on 2 February 1947, these services were numbered in the Warrington Corporation series, North Western buses displaying '10w' and '11w', as the 'true' 10 and 11 had long been used for joint routes out of Manchester. The longer-distance services into Warrington were still subject to the embargo on carrying passengers wholly within the borough, however! A beneficial provision allowed the company to base

Around two dozen of the earliest ECW-bodied Bristol L5Gs of 1946/7 had the initial version of the builder's postwar bus body, with separately glazed sliding-window ventilators and, in North Western's case, a prefabricated Clayton indicator box at the front, which features respectively made bodybuilding less reliant on craft skills and facilitated blind replacement. Seen here in its prime, No 156 is entering Bakewell, on the lengthy journey down the A6 from Buxton. *The Omnibus Society*

▲ The remainder of the 1946/7 L5Gs were more conventionally finished, with glass sliders within the overall window pans and an externally accessible coach-built indicator box. Caught *c*1951 in Parker Street, Manchester, 166 was on one of the less-remembered services via Cheadle which at that time traced a tortuous route to a residential district just east of Hazel Grove, where long layovers were often avoided by scheduling a short return trip on the 165 to Stockport. The clarity of the destination display would shame many a present-day operator. *J. W. Hillmer*

several buses and crews at the Corporation depot, which also provided support services, although peak-hour augmentation was required from Altrincham.

The company had high hopes of reviving the 1939 scheme negotiated with Stockport Corporation, but that required enabling legislation for revenue-pooling; there were greater municipal priorities, and it was not to be. The secondary town terminus at Andrew Square had remained in use for the Denton, Romiley and Mellor services until October 1946, by which time the new 400yd 'Merseyway' link had been open for six years, fuel conservation probably being the reason for the delay in moving them to Mersey Square. Ever protective, Stockport claimed a 'toll' of ¼d (0.1p) per passenger over the extension! Relationships did slowly improve, but the state of 'armed neutrality' continued to simmer, except for sensible co-operation over early and late staff buses, the Corporation covering north and west of the town, and North Western the east and south.

The winter of 1946/7 turned out to be a repeat of 1940/1, excepting the burden of the blackout, and once again services in the most exposed districts had to be suspended for at least two weeks until conditions improved. At the July 1947 AGM the Chairman was proud to announce that more than 90% of prewar route-mileage had been reinstated, expressed concern that the average age of the fleet exceeded nine years and hoped that 168 new buses would be

North Western freely used public-house names in route descriptions, and the 'Dog & Dart' near Warrington was one of the most widely known, being seen as far afield as Manchester on route 37. It is seen here on the intermediate blind of a 1946 Bristol L5G with Brush bodywork, arriving at Warrington's Bridgefoot (Arpley Station) terminus on 12 January 1957. No 102 would be sold within the year, being one of the very few of this batch not to be given a second body.
W. Ryan / Photosales

delivered by December 1948. Two years later it was revealed that a further 214 buses would arrive by the end of 1952. The best of those that remained were also going to be rejuvenated.

Back in 1947 Lambert organised vehicle exchanges in pursuance of a wish to acquire more Bristols. Six of the utility Leyland TS6s and a Guy were sent to East Midland in exchange for a 1942 K5G double-decker, plus five 1939 ECW-bodied Bristol Ls looking quite different from contemporary North Western examples, due to little more than having overhanging full-canopy roofs with a single-screen destination display! The Strachans-bodied K5G soon had five bedfellows from PMT, two being of truly austere appearance, with almost-flat roofs and extremely angular domes. The bodywork on the last was, in total contrast, a curvaceous Duple product similar to those delivered prewar to the Red & White group yet transferred unused to the Associated Bus Co of Stoke-on-Trent in 1944. In return North Western sent five of its Guys and the three Daimlers to PMT. An unexpected acquisition was of a 1939 all-Leyland TD5 returned in such a poor state by the War Department that its owner, M. Corless & Son of Coppull, near Chorley, no longer wanted it, but its thorough renovation was well within Charles Street's capabilities.

New double-deckers were the keynote for 1948/9. As Bristol was fully committed, North Western had to buy Leylands, ECW-bodied PD1As being followed by Weymann-bodied and all-Leyland PD2/1s. All had two of the new single-blind indicators, the second either at the rear or over the platform. Their vacuum-servo brakes left something to be desired, however, in later years causing drivers to overshoot by a couple of lengths the first few stops after a spell on an air-braked AEC. The Weymanns entered service alongside more all-Leyland PD2/1s, the last six, for the Manchester–Blackpool services, having platform doors, as well as luggage pens over the rear wheel-arches, with single forward-facing seats alongside. All these postwar double-deckers had not displaced any of the original 64 K5Gs, which in a new guise were to give sterling service for more than another decade.

Further rebodying in 1948 saw some stylish Weymann saloons displacing 1938 ECW bodies from Leyland Tiger chassis dating from 1934/5 and presaged the appearance of identical bodies on even more new Bristol L5G saloons in the following two years. Seven of the 1950 Bristols were the last to be ordered until 1967 and, having luggage boots, were frequently used on express work for some years. Their arrival enabled the last 19 venerable Tilling-Stevens to be honourably retired in October 1949, though rebodied Leyland Tiger petrols from 1932 would last until 1951.

The 1939 Bristol L5G/ECWs acquired from East Midland eluded most photographers before they were rebodied, but this view of 661 (later 325), on the same stand and service as 166 on page 45, shows the drastic change in appearance from the half-canopy style (see page 32) resulting from specification of an overhanging full-width front canopy. These buses could have accommodated standard three-line displays, but all seemed to be given numberless blinds, and some had prewar 'single-liners'. *Roy Marshall*

An ex-PMT K5G of 1942, with Strachans semi-utility body featuring half-drop windows, waits to get onto the 52 stand in Parker Street in 1951, a year so so before rebodying. The Manchester bus in the background is one of the half-dozen 7ft 6in-wide Crossleys of 1946/7 fitted with turbo-transmitter drive, later to be replaced with a Leyland engine and manual transmission. *J. W. Hillmer*

▲ Destination displays aside, the 10 ECW-bodied Leyland PD1As of 1948 would have looked quite at home in a Tilling company. Used initially on core services such as the 20, 52 and the Flixton group, most were eventually concentrated at Northwich, but deteriorating framework caused their demise after 13 years. No 221 is pictured *c*1950 on the same stand as No 2 (left). *J. W. Hillmer*

The 1948 all-Leyland PD2s were more durable than the ECW-bodied versions and served until 1965. With only 53-seat capacity, they were probably withdrawn more for obsolescence than any other reason. New overhead for the 210 trolleybuses, disused tram tracks and a Manchester Corporation 106 (Hyde) bus in the background date this view to 1949. Bodyside advertisements for White Chief loaves (along with those for Thom's Castile soap, Tizer soft drinks and Lanry and Wimsol bleaches) were to become almost a hallmark of NWRCC's buses in the 1950s. No 233 is pictured on the service to Ringway or Styal, worked jointly with MCTD. *J. W. Hillmer*

No 233 looked quite different in its latter-day guise, with revised destination display and livery, while, in common with the entire batch, a push-vent had very soon been added to the nearside front window on the upper deck, after vociferous passenger complaints about poor air circulation. Here it is working out its final days on a nine-minute shuttle between Sale and Ashton-on-Mersey. *F. P. Roberts*

A red roof and corner pillars detract from the stylish looks of 252, one of the Weymann-bodied PD2s delivered in 1949, and looking generally down-at-heel as it waits to depart from Uppermill for Oldham on 5 October 1961. The type's classic lines, as built, can be seen on the title page. *Ken Swallow*

'Steady as she goes'. Leyland PD2/Weymann 253 heels hard to port negotiating Oldham's Market Place roundabout on 10 March 1963 on route 10 to Greenfield, a service worked jointly with both Oldham and Manchester corporations. The bus has benefited from a heavy rebuild under Bill Leese's drive to improve maintenance standards, to an extent which kept the batch in service until 1967, but its previous good looks have been compromised in the process. *Author*

The 1950 intake was composed entirely of Bristol L types, 28 being Weymann-bodied saloons — seven with luggage boots and dual-purpose seating, the rest without boots and having bus seating. One of the latter, 303, waits on the A6 at Hazel Grove to depart on 'back-woods' route 82 to Mellor via Hawk Green and Marple in the early 1950s. *Author*

▲ One of the 1935 Leyland Tiger TS6s with its third body, a 1948 Weymann. It says much for their durability that in their 19th and final year of service these vehicles were still capable of express work on the Tyne–Tees–Mersey service. With a Coronation Year (1953) motif in its centre offside window, 671 stands next to a postwar Lancashire United Guy Arab/Roe at Wellington Street coach station, Leeds. The Weymann body would be reused successively on 1938 and 1946 Bristol L5Gs, thereby lasting until 1963. *Stan Letts*

The final batch of half-cab Bristols delivered to North Western, in 1950, is represented by Weymann-bodied L5G 311, at rest on Altrincham station forecourt in 1952. Behind it a 1936 JO5G with postwar Brush bodywork has just arrived from Macclesfield. *J. W. Hillmer*

Leyland Tiger TS4 No 579 of 1932, rejuvenated by a 1943 Burlingham utility body, shooting out from under the A6 archway and onto the parking ground behind Mersey Square bus station. The conductress, who lived in Romiley and dealt in horses when off duty, gets ready to leap off and get some 'cuppas' in from the company canteen nearby. The rear of CDB 201, a 1949 Weymann-bodied Bristol L5G, adds interest. *J. W. Hillmer*

The coach fleet at last received major attention in the years 1948-50 with the arrival of 22 new Bristol L5Gs and 10 Leyland PS2/3s, all with Windover 'Huntingdon' coachwork. Less expected was the similar rebodying of 17 prewar Leyland Tigers, still capable of reaching 60mph, but these changes did not eliminate the last prewar Harrington coaches, of which a handful were to give up to three more years' service. The Windover-bodied coaches eventually had to be withdrawn after eight years, due to structural weakness in their luggage-boot framing and behind their front bulkheads, even after their sliding roofs had been replaced by fixed panelling. It was surprising that North Western did not rebody at least the PS2s as double-deckers, as did two of BET's Yorkshire companies, but by 1958 new models with higher seating capacity within traditional 'lowbridge' overall height (13ft 6in *vs* 14ft 6in), yet with a 'passenger-friendly' highbridge upper-deck layout, were becoming available.

Ten Bristol L5G coaches bodied by Windover joined the fleet in 1949, to be followed by 12 more in 1950. The first, 261, is seen here in Altrincham bus station on 12 May 1952, its illuminated panel over the windscreen obscured by reflection. The double-decker (No 5) alongside is of particular interest, being one of the two ex-PMT K5Gs with extremely angular Strachans utility bodies, soon to be replaced by those from prewar K5G/ECWs. *J. W. Hillmer*

Ten Leyland Tiger PS2s also delivered in 1949 received identical Windover coachwork, among them 275, here giving its passengers a break at Baslow, Derbyshire, on a private hire. Parked behind it in this early-1950s scene is a Plaxton-bodied Austin CXB of Elsey's of Gosberton, Lincs, while keeping company across the road are two Sheffield 'B'-fleet Roberts-bodied AEC Regent IIIs on layover between journeys on route 37 to/from the city. *Senior Transport Archive*

In 1950 nine of the 14-year-old Harrington-bodied Leyland Tiger chassis became the final batch to be sent to Windover for rebodying. Here, in the mid-1950s, No 384 loads in Lower Mosley Street as a Tyne–Tees–Mersey duplicate as far as Leeds. With the exception of the Bristols cascaded to Melba Motors, all the Windovers would be withdrawn by the end of the decade. *Author*

No 573 was one of the six 1934 Leyland LT5A Lions with Roe bodies purchased in 1949 from sister BET company Yorkshire Woollen District. The perimeter-seating layout to which they were altered may just be discernible in this view at ICI's Winnington Works. Although serving for only three years, they plugged a gap at a critical time. *J. W. Hillmer*

Edmondson card ticket of typical railway style, presumably used for pre-booking on seasonal express services as late as 1948.

Wedded as it had been to Bristols since 1936, North Western was lucky to have been able to acquire them after the Tilling Group's sale to the British Transport Commission in 1948, due to having a large forward order sanctioned during the war by the appropriate Ministry, which the manufacturer was allowed to complete, notwithstanding (a) an embargo on Bristol sales outside the BTC after its absorption and (b) BET's centralised chassis-ordering policy. Only one other BET company, Maidstone & District, seemed able to achieve comparable success, probably for similar reasons.

Drafted in during 1949 to replace more worn-out Dennis Lancets, yet just as old, were six Leyland LT5A saloons from the Yorkshire Woollen District fleet. These were given perimeter seating primarily for use on ICI works services around Northwich, on which they were used until their demise four years later; their regular passengers doubtless accepted this retrograde step, given the prevailing circumstances. However, advantage could be taken of the extra standing capacity only within the extensive factory sites, as the legislation permitting it on public roads had been rescinded. Another unexpected event occurred within a year when six 1936 Weymann-bodied Leyland Titans from Maidstone & District turned up at Charles Street. Given very thorough overhauls, these too were consigned to Northwich garage, joining the lonely ex-Corless TD5, but did see frequent use on the 'top-link' 36 service to Altrincham and Manchester. They would be well cared for by Northwich garage's excellent maintenance standards.

A welcome sign of the relaxation of controls on equipment and supplies at around this time was the appearance of rear destination blinds in both prewar and postwar saloons and the fitting of route-number blinds in hitherto blanked-out front apertures on many utility Guys, so soon to be rebodied.

The stage was now set for much greater changes, given the company's desire to run as many Bristols as possible for the foreseeable future.

7. Maturity

The year 1950 was a watershed for the company, seeing the last new half-cab single-deckers, the start of a major rebodying programme to prolong the lives of as many pre-1947 Bristols as possible, concerted efforts to create a 'Bristol clone' specification for new chassis and, in October, an underfloor-engined Leyland Royal Tiger demonstrator with 44-seat Brush body, tested on the Manchester–Buxton service.

Chief Engineer A. S. Woodgate had moved on soon after Lambert's arrival, replaced by his East Midland successor, F. Clayton, who stayed for an even shorter period. Clayton was in turn succeeded by H. S. Driver, who arrived in time to oversee the rebuilding programme for most of the buses delivered between 1937 and 1945. The first sign, early in 1950, was the disappearance of the 21 remaining utility Guys from their normal haunts, particularly the Stockport–Bramhall–Wilmslow routes, as well as Macclesfield and Northwich services. Eight prewar Ribble Leyland Titans materialised in mid-1951, mainly on Stockport's services to Bramhall, Denton and Mellor, along with five prewar Tiger coaches from PMT, allowing work to continue also on the prewar Bristol Ks during the summer period. By then the Guys had reappeared, with slightly lower radiators and brand-new lowbridge Willowbrook bodywork, which appeared to be robust and well finished by contemporary standards. They retained their former fleet numbers.

The Guys' reappearance concealed an unforeseen sequence of events, as the plan had originally been for the Guys (presumably) and Bristols (definitely) to be rebodied by Northern Coachbuilders, of Newcastle upon Tyne. That company's recently appointed General Manager had been in charge at ECW from 1935 to 1948 and had a good rapport with North Western's senior management, having been responsible for the original bodies on the Bristol Ks and post-1934 saloons, as well as the 1948 PD1As, which the new bodies would almost certainly have resembled. However, with the contract in place and production scheduled, NCB's proprietor and major shareholder died suddenly, and liability for death duties caused the immediate cessation of bodybuilding, beyond completion of work in hand. North Western then had to find an alternative supplier with the capacity to carry out the work as closely as possible to the original plan. Willowbrook was willing, so long as it could use its own body design (much as supplied to Trent Motor Traction a year or two earlier on rebodied AEC and Daimler chassis) without having to amend it to suit a lower postwar bonnet and radiator on the Bristols. With identical bodywork to the Guys, all 64 double-deck Ks thus re-entered service in 1951/2 with their high prewar radiators but renumbered in a single batch from 400 upwards. The greatest disappointment was excessive engine noise in the lower saloon, due to the retention of rigid engine mountings.

In contrast 56 Bristol L5Gs 'recycled' in 1950/1 (including the handful of ex-East Midland saloons) all received postwar-style PV2 radiators and lowered bonnets, as well as attractive Burlingham bodywork, but were renumbered as 321-76.

Old and new bodies on the wartime Guy chassis, side-by-side at Charles Street during the rebodying programme.
Greater Manchester Transport Society

Pictured at Stockport, PMT 228, a Burlingham coach-bodied Leyland TS7 of 1935, and Ribble 1721, a Leyland TD4 of 1937, stand in for members of North Western's fleet in the summer of 1951. The destination displays on Ribble's 1930s vehicles were minuscule, in order to cram as many destinations as possible on a limited blind-length, and North Western deemed it necessary to mount a larger indicator-box under the TD4's canopy, just visible here.
Senior Transport Archive

12th MAY, 1951
Price 6d.

The next batch of 19 L5Gs reappeared in 1952, unexpectedly with Willowbrook saloon bodywork, possibly as a 'bonus order' for the bodybuilder's prompt response to the emergency with the double-deckers. These saloons were wider and longer than before and had a new, two-blind indicator layout at the front, within a standard postwar-size aperture. They also retained higher radiators and bonnets like the rebodied K5Gs, looking equally well made. Close inspection revealed that they had 38 seats, hence the slightly increased length, and were 7ft 9in wide on 7ft 6in chassis, as well as retaining their former fleet numbers, with the addition of an 'A' suffix. All the rebuilds had received very thorough chassis overhauls, including updated Gardner engines, new differentials, hubs and road springs and a revised pedal layout.

There was an equally radical change in the supply of new vehicles at this time, as 1951 saw the arrival of two examples of the recently introduced Leyland/MCW Olympic integral, with front entrance, together with two underfloor-engined Atkinson Alpha saloons, again Weymann-bodied but with rear entrances. The Atkinsons were the first examples of the marque seen on British roads as buses, although the Preston-based chassis manufacturer had an excellent reputation for its heavy lorries.

Atkinsons were purchased because of the company's inability to acquire further reliable and economical Bristols. Stuart Driver had made a determined effort to source alternative chassis using Gardner engines and other preferred components; both Foden and Atkinson had been approached, but the former had its own ideas in progress, and Atkinson eventually agreed to build a 'Bristol by proxy' to North Western's specification. Reliability turned out to be as good as expected, fuel and oil consumption being some 50% lower than that of the Olympics, resulting in an order for 14 more, for 1952 delivery. The final two were lightweight versions with Willowbrook bodies and single rear wheels, one having a four-cylinder Gardner engine which had to be replaced by a 5HLW to give adequate power. Lambert and the board agreed to standardise on Atkinsons with an order for 100, but the BET Federation was committed to a large contract for Leyland Royal Tigers, not having kept North Western's management in the picture, and refused to accede to the company's plans. On failing to get this decision reconsidered at a meeting at BET headquarters, Stuart Driver returned to Charles Street, cleared his desk and walked out, never to return.

The earliest prewar L types rebodied, by Burlingham, turned out to be quite elegant buses, due to their lower bonnets and postwar PV2 radiators. No 372 (ex 932 of 1938) waits to depart Matlock bus station in the mid-1950s, with a prewar AEC Regal of fiercely independent Silver Service (J. H. Woolliscroft) of Darley Dale alongside. *Roy Marshall*

Unexpectedly the Willowbrook versions kept the original high bonnet and radiator, even though the chassis were lengthened, to carry a 38-seat body, and widened, as can be deduced from the mudguard overhang. They also introduced a twin destination-blind layout, not used to best advantage in this 1956 shot of 869A (old number with suffix) in Hartford. *C. W. Routh*

One of the 44-seat Leyland Olympics bought to compare with the prototype Atkinsons, 396 is seen in Lower Mosley Street's lower parking area in the late 1950s. Its original livery has been slightly simplified, while behind the windscreen is a slip-board presaging a trip to Sheffield.
F. P. Roberts

An official shot of one of the prototype 'heavier-weight' Atkinsons delivered in 1951, which put in 13 years' service. After a 'honeymoon' on the 27 from Manchester to Buxton, some were based at Urmston to run with Manchester's rear-entrance Royal Tigers on the joint 22 service from Levenshulme to Eccles, to avoid stop-siting problems.
Ian Allan Library

A lightweight Atkinson of the type which, before BET intervention, North Western had hoped to make its standard underfloor-engined saloon, 1952 Willowbrook-bodied 513 had long had twin rear wheels when photographed at Urmston on a murky December day in 1961. On the left can be seen the rear of Weymann 'heavyweight' 502, from the only batch of large saloons to sport a rear destination indicator. *Author*

Loading in front of the Plaza steps in Mersey Square *c*1951, Bristol K5G No 6 (ex-East Midland) was probably the sole example to have had a route-number display on its original Strachans body. By mid-1953 it had been given a prewar ECW body. *J. W. Hillmer*

▲ A final view of a prewar Bristol K5G with an original ECW body of the type transferred to the second-hand utilities; No 887 of 1938 is seen in George Street, Piccadilly, the Manchester terminus of the 125 to Glossop since 1948 and thereafter joint with both SHMD and MCTD. Behind, a trolleybus awaits departure on the 210 service, started in 1950 to Hyde and Gee Cross. Note that the street's stone setts still embrace three disused tram tracks. *J. W. Hillmer*

The prewar 'Ls' given 1949
Weymann bodies from the
1934/5 Leylands in 1953
initially inherited the latters'
fleet numbers, hence 'new'
674/5 being formerly 866 and
928; two years later they would
be renumbered again, as 94/5.
In this view 675 has come off
a Congleton–Parker Street 52A
run, while newly repainted 674
is on the Higher Poynton–
Lower Mosley Street 32
service, both taking a breather
on the coach station's south
side. *Author*

At about this juncture Lambert retired,
to be replaced by George Brook, previously
General Manager at East Midland, although he
had also graduated through North Western.
Driver's replacement was S. J. B. Skyrme, yet
another ex-East Midland man. There were still
some unrebodied Bristols, L5G saloons and
utility Ks, and in both cases the best use was
made of existing resources. The double-
deckers re-emerged from Charles Street in
1952/3 with thoroughly rejuvenated prewar
ECW bodies, the best nine having been saved
from the 64 removed from the 'native' Ks in
the previous two years. Better still, they had
scarcely been altered in appearance apart from substitution of
conventional seating and elimination of the destination indicator
over the rear platform (and their decorative rear bumpers).
Their provenance was immediately apparent, as they perpetuated
their old fleet numbers (1-9).

For 18 of the Ls a similar tactic was employed in 1953/4 using
the Weymann saloon bodies which in 1948 had replaced the 1938
ECWs on 18 Leyland TS7s of 1935 — all very confusing, as with

many such exercises carried out by the company! This left 24 Ls
still with their original bodies, of which one was repainted
all-over red to serve as a driver-trainer, eight were stripped
for spares, 12 were sold off complete, and three were converted
to Engineering Department lorries, of which two were to
survive until 1968. The summer hires from Ribble had been
replaced in the years 1952-4 by small batches of postwar
Leyland Tigers borrowed from Yorkshire Woollen District.

Although out of strict chronological
sequence, it is appropriate to mention here
the final rebodying phase, involving the
1946 L5Gs with Brush bodies. By their 10th
year these were showing signs of distress,
yet the chassis had plenty of life left.
Accordingly 14 were rebodied with the
1949 Weymann bodies from prewar Ls,
and 19 with the 1952/3 Willowbrooks, the
balance of seven, which could not be paired
off, being sold complete, leaving the prewar
chassis to be sold with the displaced 1946
bodies, all this by 1958! The JO5Gs
rebodied by Brush in 1946 were gradually
withdrawn over the 1954-7 period also,
but the prewar Ls with postwar Burlingham
bodies continued to give sterling service
until 1961-3.

Back in the early 1950s the two Olympics
and the Atkinsons were followed by a
Leyland Royal Tiger phase, comprising
36 Weymann-bodied 44-seater saloons

Over the summers of 1952-4
the rebodying programme
was covered by hired postwar
Leyland Tigers, all Brush-
bodied PS1s from Yorkshire
Woollen District, like 608,
turning onto the parking-
ground behind Mersey Square
bus station. Note the 'Y' prefix
above the fleet number.
Willowbrook double-deckers
and an Atkinson fill in the
background, whilst a youngster
probably wonders what a
Yorkshire bus is doing in
Stockport! *J. W. Hillmer*

with standard BET Federation styling and 16 all-Leyland 41-seat coaches. The Royal Tiger coaches were capable of a good turn of speed but were heavy, both in terms of weight and on fuel, and had a vacuum-servo braking system, adequate at the time but leaving something to be desired as average traffic speed and density increased, eventually leading to their withdrawal in 1962/3, when their second Certificates of Fitness became due, as they could not safely achieve the faster timings demanded by motorway services. Originally in a smart livery of off-white with red window-frames, they were arguably to suffer from more detail alterations than any other type in the fleet: by the time of their withdrawal very few had exactly the same appearance, as brightwork was altered, removed or overpainted, according to the trim-supply situation at the time of overhauls or accident repairs. A 50:50 red (lower panels) and black version was particularly dire, soon losing its gloss, yet paradoxically suited Midland Red vehicles well!

In 1954 BET began to allocate to North Western successive batches of Leyland Tiger Cubs and then — to everyone's surprise

(and presumably for comparison) — a quartet of AEC's rival Reliance model, which externally could be differentiated only by an additional ventilation grille in the front panels, for better brake cooling. On the coaching front the same policy prevailed, but four Tiger Cubs received the recently introduced Burlingham 'Seagull' design, whereas a lone Reliance bore the very first example of Weymann's 'Fanfare', gaining it a place at the 1954 Commercial Motor Show. By this time there had also been some new double-deckers, in the shape of a lone all-Leyland PD2/10 in 1952 and six PD2/12s with attractive Weymann bodywork in 1953, which raised false hopes of improving standards in having a route indicator over the platform as well as front and rear. After the Atkinsons all underfloor-engined saloons were equipped with a single-line destination indicator at the front only, accompanied by a triple-track route number display, but at least the blinds included many more destinations than hitherto, including those appropriate to specific works and schools services.

It came as little surprise when, in 1952/3, North Western emulated Ribble in acquiring some stylish all-Leyland Royal Tiger coaches with an alternative livery styling which suited them equally well. No 608 was photographed when brand-new on 10 July 1952 at Blackpool's Coliseum coach station. In the background can be seen a pair of West Yorkshire Bristol Ls and a Ribble 'White Lady' Leyland PD1 awaiting their next spells of duty. *J. W. Hillmer*

As late as July 1958 the company had no qualms in using service buses on long express runs, demonstrated here by 1953 Royal Tiger/Weymann 517 in Liverpool, ready to depart on the inter-worked X97/X2 service to Nottingham. In 1955 even rebodied prewar Bristols were still being used as duplicates on the Tyne–Tees–Mersey expresses! *Ken Swallow*

No 557 was amongst the company's first AEC Reliances, being one of the quartet delivered in 1954. About to turn into Stamford New Road from Kingsway (a street since obliterated by redevelopment), it is pictured leaving Altrincham for Knutsford on the 38 in 1963. Note the subtle change in shape of the front dome from that of the 1953 Royal Tigers. *Author*

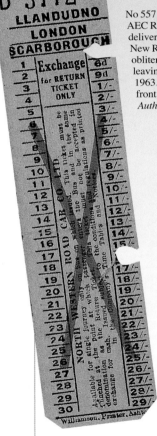

High-value exchange ticket for express services, *c*1952.

A location rarely featured yet visited by hundreds of buses every day, Stockport's St Petersgate forms the backdrop for this photograph taken *c*1959 of North Western 554, one of a batch of six Leyland PD2/12s new in 1953 with well-designed Weymann bodywork. Although still in original livery it has already had its over-platform indicator taken out of use. *A. Moyes*

By 1955 the company was well into a steady intake of Leyland's lighter Tiger Cub model. They looked much better in their original livery, which 1955-built 594 still wore when snapped at Knoll Green on the Altrincham–Mobberley–Wilmslow 96 service. *C. W. Routh*

The company bought the very first Weymann Fanfare-bodied coach, which prior to delivery was displayed at the 1954 Commercial Motor Show. At first having only a single, central destination panel, AEC Reliance 570 had been fitted with a revised display upon overhaul. Just visible on the left is a Duple Donington-bodied Reliance coach from the Rochdale-based Yelloway fleet. *Photobus*

Ready for a works journey from Buxton Market Place in 1967, its penultimate year of service, 585 also represents the large intake in the mid-1950s of underfloor-engined buses with BET Federation-style bodies by Weymann.
In spite of its excellent appearance it would meet its demise at the hands of a Barnsley breaker just two years later. *Author*

Opportunities to expand bus services after wartime cutbacks had been restored were limited mainly to serving new housing. Construction of the Bridge Hall Estate at Adswood in the early 1950s resulted in yet another stand-off with Stockport over applications for separate services, resolved only by the Traffic Commissioners' granting both in 1952! An exception had been the 125 service from Glossop to Hyde, which had been extended into Manchester to replace the Corporation's limited-stop service (8) in November 1948, following which the Corporation shared the whole of the 125 with North Western and SHMD.

A fruitful source of expansion lay in express services, the company making even greater efforts in this field by introducing more direct services to popular resorts — particularly for 'Wakes Weeks', if not for the whole summer season — and also by extending services from Derby and Nottingham to Manchester through to Blackpool or even Liverpool and, in the other direction, to Skegness or Great Yarmouth. Links such as these were sometimes introduced before being officially licensed, by allowing staff to drive other companies' coaches, Trent's running north of Manchester, and Ribble's south, 'on hire' to North Western, without the need for through-booked passengers to alight. In 1954, following the takeover by Ribble and Western SMT of Glasgow-based Northern Roadways, a through service from Coventry to Glasgow was achieved, operated jointly by North Western and Midland Red, in recognition of these companies' territorial interests in the southern section.

Another initiative was the introduction *c*1952 of Coach-Air services, whereby, for at least 10 years, through bookings to the Isle of Man were offered in co-ordination with Lancashire Aircraft Corporation Ltd (and its successors), appropriate Blackpool express services making a minor diversion into Squires Gate Airport at the resort. A natural extension of this

principle later saw the introduction of through bookings via the steamer services to the Island. By the end of the 1950s this strategy had expanded from increasing the range of destinations to increasing further the points of origin and was successful in retaining traffic that might have been lost sooner to the private car. It may also have been of marginal benefit in reducing congestion at peak holiday nodal points such as Lower Mosley Street, where in the 1950s queues on a Saturday could almost encircle the main buildings, impeding neighbourhood traffic; indeed, the first Saturday of the Manchester Engineering Holidays (around 21 July each year) was always viewed with trepidation, being referred to by staff as 'Black Saturday'.

Whilst in many cases — usually at the instigation of the railway authorities — the Traffic Commissioners imposed strict limits on express-service duplication these often seemed to be honoured more in the breach than the observance, and a service such as Manchester–Bridlington–Scarborough, running only two or three times each week, might sometimes have over 50 coaches for a 'single' Saturday departure, the majority being hired in from

small operators around the region. Company garages would be scoured for every possible bus and coach, resulting in frenzied workshop activity (and dire consequences if any were unjustifiably withheld). At the busiest weekends even office staff holding PSV licences would be sent out to drive, if only to get vehicles in position on the Friday evening! Many a service bus would be allocated to express duties (the rear seats being used for luggage stowage where necessary), including even the 100-mile trip to Scarborough!

On services like Manchester–Blackpool double-deckers hired from the Manchester and SHMD municipal fleets were commonplace on the busiest Saturdays, and as late as the 1955 railway strike North Western hired prewar SHMD Daimlers, even for the Liverpool service; these were, at least, a better proposition than the rebodied prewar Bristol K5Gs, which continued to be so used until their demise in July 1965! Conversely, coaches were often used to duplicate commuter runs to and from Manchester, before or after their express duties.

One of the 1946 Bristol Ls rebodied in 1957/8 with the 7ft 9in-wide Willowbrook saloons, 273 stands on the forecourt of Altrincham railway station in August 1963, ready to work a local journey to Briony Avenue on a new 199 service. The clock tower dominated the scene before the transport interchange was built on this site. *Author*

Pictured in the late 1950s, Bristol K5G No 456 of 1939, by now with its second body, leaves Preston's Lord's Walk coach station on an X60 to Blackpool — a trying journey for crew and passengers alike. On the left Ribble 'White Lady' Leyland PD2 No 1245 has called in on the X4 route to Burnley, whilst on the right a West Yorkshire Bristol L/ECW pulls out for Bradford — all observed by a group of keen 'bus spotters'. *Ken Swallow*

8. Indian Summer

During the early 1950s the search for economies had started in earnest as operating costs escalated ever faster, accompanied by a rapid succession of fares increases, four having occurred by 1957. By then the graduated increases successively applied across the board had thrown up many anomalies, and the Commissioners asked that fares be more closely related to mileage in future revisions. This was particularly difficult to apply where joint services were concerned, as fares in different operators' areas were not necessarily set on a consistent basis. The general rule was that the operator with the greater proportion of mileage for each particular cross-boundary fare should set it. With three or more operators, as on the 10 (Manchester–Oldham–Greenfield) or the 20/20A (Manchester–Stockport–Poynton/Woodford), the same principle applied, but the complications multiplied, and on the latter route the alternative outer termini were quite different distances from the point of divergence, altering the proportionate mileages! Where journeys in opposite directions used some different roads, then the average distance was used, and the same had to apply where two services had common sections between the same termini but where one was significantly longer than the other, as on the 7 and 8 between Stockport and Macclesfield, the first running direct via Adlington, the second indirect via Bollington.

The company then decided to alter the ground-rules and apply differing fare scales according to the viability of each route or part-route, creating 'A', 'B', and 'C' scales for profitable, break-even and loss-making stretches respectively. Firstly the fare tables had to be re-written to show the mileage between every fare stage, without exceeding the total route mileage, before a start could be made on entering and cross-checking the individual fares. The worst case was route 4 from Buxton to Derby, on which by the early 1960s there were well over 500 fares that needed calculation by North Western, not counting those that were joint operator Trent's responsibility. Even on NWRCC's own services this task could be daunting; for example the 27 from Manchester to Buxton had MCTD fares to Levenshulme, Stockport's to Great Moor, NWRCC 'A' scale to New Mills, 'B' scale to Horwich End, 'C' scale to Buxton Golf Club and 'B' scale for the final stretch to Buxton Market Place. Given that there were 212 routes that needed checking against each other (to ensure that the fare between any two common points was the same by all reasonable routes), the task was monumental!

In the meantime the engineers had been considering their options, one of the first, tried in the 1954-6 period, being the use on some saloons of single (rather than twin) rear wheels — an experiment that was soon concluded due to lack of adhesion. At around the same time Bristol L5G/ECW 145 was spray-painted all-over red (probably an S. J. B. Skyrme initiative), giving it a very dismal appearance, which, fortunately, was repeated later only on two or three 44-seat saloons. Soon afterwards a number of the Brush-bodied JO5Gs were given red roofs (tolerable, if not an improvement), and this treatment was gradually extended. In the meantime the rest of the fleet kept its smart traditional livery of red lower panels and off-white upperworks, exceptions being two Weymann-bodied Bristol L5Gs and an all-Leyland Titan, which in the mid-1950s appeared in a livery of cherry-red with a single white band. Although presentable, this would not be applied to saloons until the 1960s, and then in the standard shade of red, and without the black lining separating the colours.

Another tactic was to try alternative vehicles, and in 1954 a Bedford SBO with Duple Midland MoD-style body and a Saunders-Roe-bodied Guy LUF were both evaluated on the Manchester–Buxton route, without result. Ten AEC Reliances arrived in 1955 with Burlingham bus bodies (basically to get round a full MCW order book) and single rear wheels. They seemed flimsier than their Weymann-bodied contemporaries and, being equally disliked by platform staff and engineers, were passed from garage to garage on the slightest pretext. The 'lightweight' policy was further extended by a 1956 delivery of 10 Leyland PD2s with Weymann 'Orion'-style bodies, the Company's last double-deckers of traditional lowbridge layout — and truly awful from a conductor's viewpoint. A combination of platform doors, a wide pillar at the nearside rear corner and relatively small windows with thick pillars ensured that visibility for 'ringing off' from stops was severely restricted, even from the rear platform, and collectively they must have been the cause of

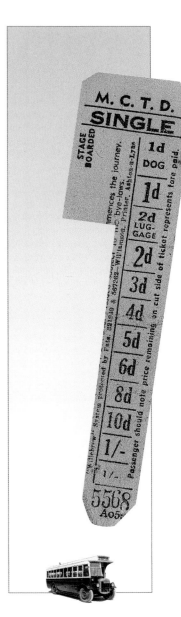

All-Leyland PD2/1 No 230, in its experimental livery of cherry red and white, on the Hayfield stand at Lower Mosley Street in the mid-1950s. *Author*

Similar treatment was meted out to 1946 Bristol L5G saloon 103 in 1957, when it was rebodied with a Weymann 35-seater from a prewar Leyland and renumbered 98.
It is seen here in 1958 at Halebarns on a 40 circular, with a trip from Altrincham to the 'Petrochemicals' works at Carrington to follow. From memory, the driver's name was Whittaker. *Author*

In August 1954 the company took the unorthodox step of trying out a Bedford SBO with MoD-style bodywork on the prestige Buxton–Manchester service, in this shot caught city-bound on the A6 (Wellington Road North) at Heaton Chapel. *Author*

North Western's 10 Burlingham-bodied AEC Reliances had a distinctive, non-BET character, dictated by a full order book at Weymann's Addlestone works. They gained a poor reputation (braking aside) with staff yet still served a full 13-year spell. No 619 is seen in Matlock bus station in the early 1960s on the Wirksworth service. *Photobus*

numerous boarding accidents. Furthermore, unless fully laden they shook crew and passengers alike, the suspension being unsuited to the lightweight bodywork. They featured yet another indicator layout, with the addition of a separate three-track number display alongside a front two-blind destination box, but no indicators were fitted to sides or rear.

Lightweight specification reached its nadir with six Weymann-bodied Albion Aberdonian 42-seaters delivered in 1957. These were akin to Tiger Cubs but had lighter chassis and bodies and O.400 engines, redeemed through being coupled to five-speed gearboxes rather than the four-speed of the Tiger Cubs. The first Aberdonians to enter service in the UK, they left something to be desired in terms of performance but, saved by low-ratio back axles, lasted for 10 years, exiled to the hilly routes worked from Oldham after a 'honeymoon' at other garages.

Problems arose with Stockport (again) following a 1952 boundary extension incorporating Bredbury and Romiley, where the Corporation developed a large overspill housing estate at Brinnington, close to North Western's long-established 81 Denton service. In the early stages the company met demand by short-

workings to the estate, secure under the umbrella of a clause in the Extension Order that Stockport would not encroach on any route not previously authorised. Needless to say, as development progressed, the Corporation applied for consent under Section 101 of the 1930 Road Traffic Act to run its buses in the additional area. It was then declared that the 1952 Extension Order was defective in law, and the Ministry of Transport advised the Traffic Commissioners to bar Stockport's buses from the area. The Corporation did not take this without demur, and further legal process ensued to the point where the two operators saw greater benefit in agreeing to joint working rather than in yet more litigation, co-ordination at last being implemented in December 1957.

By this time North Western's acquisition trail was almost at an end, but 1958 saw the takeover of two modest coaching concerns in the Manchester area, both of which would continue to operate under their own names for nine years. One was Reddish-based Melba Motors, long noteworthy for exotic fleet variety, which had included Foden two-stroke, Daimler, AEC and Crossley chassis and Bellhouse-Hartwell, Yorkshire Yachtbuilders and

The same bus in its final months, running 'dead' down the recently opened Exchange Street towards Stockport bus station in May 1971, having come off the Marple–Hazel Grove service and looking somewhat the worse for wear. *Author*

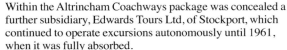

At first glance the Albion Aberdonians looked no different from the many Leyland Tiger Cubs and AEC Reliances entering the fleet in the mid-1950s, but the front wheels gave the game away, as did the badge on the dash. No 718 is seen in Delph. *F. P. Roberts*

Pearson coachwork. Some had already disappeared, and seven were acquired but not operated. They were initially replaced by obsolete Bristol/Windover coaches and some Tiger Cub/'Seagulls', because Melba had been in financial straits when taken over. The remaining fleet was non-standard and in need of extensive overhaul, and NWRCC was unsure as to whether the operation could be returned to profit. Its staple traffic consisted of school journeys crossing the boundaries between Manchester and Stockport, along with work for non-Education Authority schools. Other than on summer Saturdays, when all coaches were commandeered for express augmentation, North Western also made the best of new excursion opportunities afforded from Reddish, Gorton and Denton, which soon made a valuable contribution to the bottom line.

Whilst excursion and private-hire work was important to the other company, Altrincham Coachways, it also operated seasonal expresses to Abergele and Blackpool, using Plaxton-bodied Bedfords and older Crossleys (with Santus and TransUnited bodies) which were not acquired in the deal, and it immediately gained some nearly new Tiger Cub coaches. It also differed in being a partial takeover, as its manager retained a significant shareholding — and was emphatic that his coaches would not disappear on North Western duplication every summer Saturday!

Within the Altrincham Coachways package was concealed a further subsidiary, Edwards Tours Ltd, of Stockport, which continued to operate excursions autonomously until 1961, when it was fully absorbed.

In 1960 Melba Motors and Altrincham Coachways were each allocated a pair of new AEC Reliances with Willowbrook Viscount coachwork, later to be followed by better 'hand-me-downs'. In the case of Altrincham Coachways North Western made an uncharacteristic purchase, in 1961, of eight new petrol-engined Bedford SB3s with Duple bodywork, five of which eventually migrated to Reddish. In 1967 Melba was wound up, and Altrincham Coachways was sold to the Godfrey Abbott Group, in Sale.

Almost the final takeover of a scheduled operation was effected in 1959, when A. E. Bowyer & Son Ltd of Northwich was acquired for £1,500. A seasonal express service from Northwich to Liverpool was continued, along with excursions and tours from Northwich and Knutsford. The same year also saw the introduction, in conjunction with Crosville, of a new seasonal express service from the Sandbach area to North Wales; in addition, part of the Manchester–London service was re-routed onto newly opened sections of the M1, and that December a limited-stop service to Alderley via the new Kingsway bypass was instituted, jointly with Manchester Corporation, the latter regaining access to this territory by virtue of a new overspill estate at Handforth.

Scarcely had the Brinnington issue been resolved in 1957 than the focus of attention turned to Biddulph, a town which PMT had never accepted as being a territorial boundary. North Western had long been unhappy about penetrating services run by W. S. Rowbotham of Harriseahead and Wells' Motor Services of Biddulph, the latter having been acquired by PMT in 1953, though still run autonomously to avoid disturbing the uneasy truce between the two major companies. This eventually became an inconvenience to PMT, and in January 1959 it was fully absorbed, after prior discussion with North Western, at which it was further agreed that Biddulph should be reclassified as a 'border town' [1].

---

1. These pedantic legal niceties were actually the terms used in both letter and formal agreements, 'common town' denoting one in which each company had the right to start new services in any direction, without reference to the other, whereas 'border town' indicated an agreed boundary between two companies, which could not be violated by unilateral service extensions by either company into the territory of the other, unless by mutual agreement and/or joint operation.

North Western garage facilities at Biddulph had until this time amounted to little more than a dormy shed in Well Street plus a parking area for a few more, latterly with two old buses for staff accommodation, although land had been bought in August 1939 for a proper structure to be built in Walley Street. As part of the discussions of 1957/8 it was agreed that, due to the town's proximity to PMT's HQ in Stoke, the land should be sold for a nominal sum to the latter, which would build a permanent garage to house the buses of both operators and provide all maintenance and administration facilities at cost, and that platform staff could be used on each other's services in case of emergency. Furthermore, it was accepted by both sides that (a) established services crossing Biddulph town centre should continue to be operated solely by the initiating company, (b) new town services should be jointly operated and (c) new projecting services might be independently or jointly operated, by mutual agreement. It was further agreed that there should be a final settlement of other outstanding issues, complicated by PMT's purchase in January 1959 of Rowbotham's, whose services had continued even where competing with those of either of the two BET companies. Perhaps it was a sign of the times that North Western did not display its characteristic haste to get around the negotiating table in this era of declining traffic, and for one reason or another matters were not fully resolved until 1963. In the meantime the new garage was opened in August 1960, heralding an arrangement that was to work well for both parties.

Batches of new Leyland saloons had continued to arrive at Charles Street until 1960, followed by AECs, both in bus and coach form. Towards the end of 1957 Weymann bus styling was altered to a smoother outline, but in 1958 Willowbrook managed to gain BET's major order, producing a bodyshell which was pure BET and again more upright in appearance, but both designs were given more-comfortable seating and an attractive new three-colour livery, looking the part for limited-stop services.
The extra colour was black, from roof to waistrail,

One of the Bristol/Windovers transferred to Melba Motors as a stopgap from 1958 to 1960, signed for a trip to London — somewhat improbably, unless on an excursion there.
Roy Marshall

Rebodied Bristol K5G 428 of 1939 pulls out of Well Street, Biddulph, whilst working the 25 to Congleton in October 1961. It would continue to serve for three more years.
A. Moyes

A pleasant surprise in 1957 was the unexpected black, cream, and red dual-purpose livery of that year's Weymann-bodied AEC Reliances, which really enhanced their appearance. No 733, still pristine, loads for Derby at Lower Mosley Street in December 1961. *Author*

Still in the three-tone dual-purpose livery, AEC Reliance/Willowbrook 758 of 1958 sweeps out of Lord's Walk coach station in Preston on an X9 Oldham–Blackpool working in August 1965. Loading at the stands are a Ribble Leyland PD3/Burlingham and Royal Tiger saloon. *Author*

but a cream waistband above red lower panels made all the difference and was applied to deliveries as late as 1961. Exceptionally, 10 of the 1959 Willowbrooks had been painted in all-over cream, relieved by just a red waistband, and equipped with full coach seats, to meet a shortage of proper coaches, and both versions were sometimes drafted onto even the London services, accepted without demur by crews and passengers alike. However, even as the last were delivered in the three-tone colour scheme, the first were being demoted by the application of a red-roofed bus livery. The 'pure' coaches had been sourced from Weymann and Burlingham ('Fanfares' and 'Seagulls' respectively) until 1958, but there was a switch to Harrington in 1959 and then to Willowbrook the following year.

▲ Leyland Tiger Cub/Willowbrook 772, also a 1958 delivery, represents the exceptional cream-with-red-band livery in Cleveleys in April 1962, while on a layover on the X69 from Hyde, Ashton, and Oldham. It would pass to Crosville in 1972 for two more years' service. *Author*

▲ Arriving at Cleveleys in August 1965 on the X36 from Sharston and Altrincham, a sister vehicle demonstrates the red-roof livery to which many eventually succumbed. A Ribble inspector, having told the driver where to park, looks on disapprovingly. *Author*

One of the last Weymann Fanfare coaches acquired, Reliance 744 of 1958 is seen three years later on Elizabeth Bridge in London, awaiting a call from Victoria Coach Station (in the background) to collect its passengers for the X5 to Manchester. *Author* ▶

In the 1950s there had been several more demonstrators, including an all-Leyland PD2 (NTF 9) on the 125 in 1952, an underfloor-engined Dennis Lancet in 1954 and, in 1955, Leyland's revolutionary rear-engined, rear-entrance double-decker (STF 90), precursor to the Atlantean, which ran on the 28 from Manchester to Hayfield — a radical change from the usual fare of throbbing Bristol K5Gs! In 1959 one of the six-year-old (550-series) Leyland PD2s was experimentally fitted with an air-cooled Ruston & Hornsby engine and a wider, home-made 'tin-front' bonnet, which spoiled its appearance. Not successful enough in this application, it was restored to its previous condition at next overhaul. In the interim the experiment was repeated with a 1963 AEC Reliance, with the same result.

By 1960 the writing was really on the wall, requiring drastic survival measures. The fuel shortages caused by the 1956 Suez crisis had reduced service levels and thereby patronage whilst increasing costs for a significant period, and a nine-day strike over wages across the company side of the industry in July 1957 inevitably caused further loss of traffic. The growth of private motoring had begun to cause serious road congestion beyond peak hours, causing leisure traffic to fall off noticeably, and the duplication once regularly required on Sundays on services to Buxton, Hayfield, Lyme Park and similar destinations was becoming exceptional. In 1960 the crunch intensified with an 11% increase in the wages bill caused by having to concede a reduction in the standard working week from 44 to 42 hours, plus a significant increase in basic rates, altogether imposing about £170,000 on costs in a full year, after protracted negotiations with trades unions. By that time wages had long since exceeded 50% of total costs; half the services and a third of the total mileage were not meeting operating costs, even though conversion to one-man operation of buses had been progressing steadily since April 1958. A brighter note lay in the loyalty of 305 staff who had notched up at least 25 years of service.

Operating efficiencies were improved in several ways, such as converting local services from out-and-back runs into cross-town links with no layovers in the bus station. This was taken a stage further in Buxton, where three short, half-hourly services with common departure times from the Market Place were rescheduled to leave in succession at 10-minute intervals, which enabled four buses and eight crews to cover work previously needing six buses and 12 crews. Economies were extended to the Warrington 'arrangement', Altrincham crews being sent out 'on the cushions', by the earliest 37 departure, to pick up their buses at the Corporation depot; at mid-day replacement crews and buses worked out on successive timings, the early-shift crews and their vehicles picking up the return trips, the late crews parking up at the WCT depot to return as passengers — a stratagem which overall saved 22 miles of dead-running a day per bus outstationed. On express work there was a chance to make some useful savings by mutual assistance if there were heavy one-way flows in opposing directions for two companies, 'Stockport Wakes' (NWRCC) out to Blackpool, and 'Hanley Feast' (PMT) back, for instance.

A further problem lay in the time-lag between applications for fares increases and their approval, which was by no means a foregone conclusion, being vociferously opposed by many statutory objectors. By March 1960 profits tax had increased from 3% to 12% in less than three years, and over 10 years fuel duty had increased from 2.5p to 12.5p per gallon, some £231,000 having just been paid to the Exchequer in 12 months on that score alone. In marginal ways also the tide had turned against the company, an example being the proliferation of bodywork styles, which required a much greater stockholding of vulnerable items like front- and rear-light bezels, bumpers and glazing, as well as mechanical components. Pressure to reduce spares stock meant reliance on prompt replenishment from manufacturers, and there were regular instances of buses being kept out of service for days at a time when this was not readily forthcoming.

The glory days were certainly over for North Western, and it was now a case of managing decline.

NORTH WESTERN ROAD CAR CO. LTD.

Express and Limited Stops

COMMENCING 19th MAY 1961 until 24th SEPTEMBER 196

ADSWOOD (GREYHOUND)-	MOBBERLEY POST OFFICE-
ALDERLEY (THE CIRCUIT)-	MOBBERLEY (RAJAR WORKS)-
ALDERLEY (DISTRICT BANK)-	NOON SUN CORNER-
ALDERLEY PARK (I.C.I.)-	OVERSLEY BANK-
MACCLESFIELD-	PARRS WOOD-
MANCHESTER (L.M.S.)-	PRESTBURY (LEGH ROAD)-
MANCHESTER (PICCADILLY)-	PRESTBURY FOLD-
MANCHESTER (CHORLTON STREET)-	STOCKPORT-
WILMSLOW-	UPTON PRIORY ESTATE-
ALTRINCHAM-	WHIRLEY BARN-
BELMONT-	WILMSLOW-
BRAMHALL-	WILMSLOW STATION-
	SCHOOL SERVICE-
BUXTON-	SHOWGROUND-
CHEADLE (P.O.)-	PRIVATE-
CHEADLE (WHITE HART)-	EXCURSION-
CHEADLE HULME (WARREN ROAD)-	
CROSS ROAD (BOLSHAW ROAD)-	ASHTON-
GREAT WARFORD-	BLACKPOOL-
MACCLESFIELD-	BRADFORD-
GRIFFIN HOTEL-	BRIDLINGTON-
HALEBARNS-	CLEVELEYS-
HANDFORTH (W.&H.)-	COLWYN BAY-
	DERBY-
HEALD GREEN STATION-	FILEY (BUTLIN'S CAMP)-
KERRIDGE-	GLOSSOP-
SHAW HEATH-	HYDE-
KNUTSFORD-	LEEDS-
KNUTSFORD (LILAC AVENUE)-	LIVERPOOL-
WILMSLOW-	LLANDUDNO-
WILMSLOW STATION-	MANCHESTER-
BROOK LANE CORNER-	NORTHWICH-
COLSHAW FARM-	NOTTINGHAM-
DAVENPORT GREEN-	OLDHAM-
GRAVEL LANE (CUMBER LANE)-	RHYL-
LACEY GREEN ESTATE-	SCARBOROUGH-
LINDOW END-	WYTHENSHAWE-
	EXPRESS SERVICE-
	NORTH WESTERN-

A 1960s single-deck blind for Wilmslow garage, with Midland Red-style 'W' code alongside each display, and express destination series for summer weekend duplication.

In 1959 a Dennis Loline in Aldershot & District's striking livery of two-tone-green and cream provided a contrast with the warmer hues in Mersey Square. Almost a Bristol, being built under licence for operators outside the BTC and combining a Gardner engine and lowbridge height, the Loline had normal seating and a central gangway upstairs, with no ceiling intrusion in the lower saloon, and rear air suspension. Of instant appeal to platform staff, engineers, and accountants alike (all the company's double-deckers since 1931 having had a sunken offside gangway with four-abreast seating upstairs), it led to orders for 15 for delivery in 1960 and 35 more in 1961/2. Although the demonstrator from A&D had a conventional rear entrance (with platform doors), North Western's were given forward entrances, in line with contemporary trends.

The initial batch of Lolines were Mk II models bodied by East Lancashire Coachbuilders (another new departure), the majority being specified with the thirstier option of a Leyland O.600 engine, and just three with the new Gardner 6LX, which was then an unknown quantity. Although heavier than their successors, the East Lancs bodies soon seemed to rattle excessively and develop an unkempt appearance, due to reduced maintenance standards. The larger group of 1961/2 (Loline IIIs) arrived with yet another option, Alexander bodywork; all had Gardner 6LX engines, and 25 had five-speed gearboxes, for inter-urban work. Having convinced BET that it could produce a durable and competitively priced product, Alexander became an approved supplier for saloons also, North Western ordering 20 bodies on AEC Reliance chassis for 1961 and a further 10 to the newly permitted 36ft length on Leyland Leopard chassis for 1962. The outcome of a policy decision to cascade coaches to bus duties later in their lives, these bodies were bus shells finished internally to coach standards, with additional glazing in the roof coving above the side windows.

To enable them to react more quickly to local circumstances, depot inspectors were from 1960 given greater autonomy, also becoming responsible for drivers, hitherto under the jurisdiction and day-to-day control of the Chief Engineer's department. In the days of crew operation it had been general practice for drivers to move down a garage's roster and conductors to move up it, on a weekly basis, apart from three weeks each year, so that even long-service staff worked as a pair for no more than a week at a time for 49 out of 52 weeks. To add further variety, even a day's shift usually took crews onto more than one route, often using very different buses. This appealed to many, who regarded the few duties spent solely on a local service (like the 25-minute Timperley or Halebarns circulars in Altrincham, for example) as a hardship. It certainly made better use of crews and vehicles, albeit at the expense of vehicle condition, for no-one would report a minor fault or accident damage if a changeover were scheduled within the hour. An exception was a two-bus dormy shed at Castleton, in the Peak District, where one vehicle operated a shuttle to Hope station, the other the company's share of the jointly operated 72 to Sheffield. The buses would alternate day-about, and as that on the 72 met the 84 from Buxton to Sheffield the crews exchanged vehicles, enabling the Castleton one to return to Buxton for refuelling and minor repairs. One-man operation was the only way to keep such rural services operating for a few more years. Although this was strongly opposed in principle by the trades union, the 15% pay premium induced many drivers to go against union advice, as they realised that their services would be decimated if OMO were not adopted.

Discussions on the outstanding Wells/Rowbotham issues in Biddulph commenced at Charles Street in January 1962 between the two Traffic Managers, by then Derek Fytche for NWRCC and Robert Bailey for PMT. The upshot was that North Western joined in operation of the summer-only Harriseahead–Blackpool service, incorporating both one established in the 1950s from nearby Knypersley and a PMT express from Chell Heath. The Stockport company was also to participate in the seasonal service from Harriseahead to Llandudno, having just gained licences to run there from Congleton in summer peaks. After some hesitation PMT agreed to through joint-working between Congleton and Mow Cop via Biddulph and eventually handed over school and works services from Congleton to Sandbach Grammar School and to Foden's works at Elworth.

Two of the 1960 Dennis Lolines with East Lancs bodies on the 28 in Stockport when new — 813, with Gardner 6LX engine, inbound to the city, and 816, with Leyland O.600 engine, outbound to Hayfield; both would later pass to SELNEC, which would soon withdraw them. In the background a 1947 Stockport Crossley loads on the Corporation's Adswood stand. *Dennis Gill*

The Lolines' appearance was not improved by a subsequent reduction of the destination display. Ironically in this March 1966 view of 816 on the 14 to Uppermill via Lees, being hustled through Oldham Market Place by a Corporation Leyland PD2, the driver has made the best of an old three-line blind behind a single-line destination aperture.
Note also the illuminated offside advertisement panel, fitted to the entire batch from new. *Author*

▲ A further shot on the 14 shows 895 in full flight in Ashton Road, Oldham, in July 1968. The third and final batch of Lolines — Alexander-bodied Mk III models of 1962 — would be split between SELNEC and Crosville in January 1972. Some, including 895, had five-speed gearboxes for inter-urban work. *Author*

Loline III/Alexander 880 offloading at Blackpool's Coliseum coach station after a trip from Manchester at Easter 1969. The usual scrum of arrivals also includes an LUT Guy Arab, Ribble PD3s and an Atlantean and another North Western Loline. On occasion drivers of Lolines from the southernmost garages were heard to ask duty inspectors to "Give her a rest before you send her back"! *Peter Makinson*

There were other minor adjustments, and PMT was allowed to keep the ex-Wells service from Hanley to Winsford (Over) without prejudice to North Western's interests north of Sandbach. By this time the Road Car was keen to resolve the problem of the unremunerative service from Knutsford to Holmes Chapel, wishing to link this with PMT's Hanley–Manchester limited-stop, but this fell on fallow ground, as did PMT's hope of sharing North Western's aspirations to extend a Manchester–Biddulph service to the Potteries. As PMT had had the benefit of acquiring all the Wells fleet in 1953, North Western did not pay any goodwill for participation in the relevant services, but the sale of the land for Biddulph garage at little more than a token price was some compensation. Additionally £1,250 was paid to PMT as goodwill for the element of ex-Rowbotham services acquired.

Just to keep the Traffic Department on its toes, a 'Brinnington situation' recurred about this time, involving a large Manchester

Corporation overspill housing estate planned for Hattersley, just off the 125 route between Hyde and Mottram. Its traffic potential was far more desirable than dwindling patronage around Congleton and Biddulph, and North Western was prepared to fight for it. However, Manchester excluded North Western by commencing a joint service to the city with SHMD, as a progressive diversion of up to half the former 210 trolleybus service to nearby Gee Cross, which had been converted to motor bus in April 1963. North Western's interference caused postponement for 10 months of the Hattersley–Manchester element, which eventually started only as a peak-hour connection, with a very tortuous routeing through Hyde to minimise overlapping of the 125, and, emphasising the point, was even given the one-time tram-service number 19!

Further fleet variety came as the 1960s progressed, in the form of more long saloons that almost matched the capacity of traditional double-deckers. An initial delivery of 35 Willowbrook-

The Alexander bodywork phase started in 1961, the bus shells of the initial 20 being fitted out as coaches, emphasised here by AEC Reliance 845 parked on Elizabeth Bridge over London's Victoria station, awaiting its turn to be called to the Manchester X5M stand in the nearby coach station, when new. Note the short-lived 'compass' logo on the side panel. *Author*

One of the batch repainted after five years for dual-purpose work, seen on the 92 from Wilmslow to Knutsford soon after transfer to PTE operation, the brown SELNEC (Cheshire) logo on the cab side panel not showing up against North Western's red paintwork. *P. J. Thompson*

bodied AEC Reliances in 1963 was followed by regular injections of Leyland Leopards with Alexander Y-type bodywork. However, after the Lolines the double-deck intake was more radical, including 30 forward-entrance AEC Renowns interspersed in 1963/4 with up-to-date Daimler Fleetlines (the former bodied by Park Royal, the latter by Alexander), which type prevailed until delivery of a final 10 in 1967. Prior to the advent of the Fleetlines, LUT 97 and Birmingham 3246 had been tried out on the 28 to Hayfield, in comparison with a Trent Leyland Atlantean.

The arrival in 1962, from Trent, of new General Manager William Leese brought about a determined effort to restore the company's maintenance standards, which had begun to attract the attention of Ministry Vehicle Examiners. It led to a general smartening-up of the fleet, standardisation of livery application and conversions to a universal indicator layout, even some of the old K5Gs being given a single-line destination blind above a three-track number display. This greatly reduced makeshift arrangements — brought about by mismatches between the (frequent) reallocation of buses and the availability locally of appropriate destination blinds — as well as saving miles of black masking tape and minimising journeys to 'Duplicate'. Almost all buses looked better for it, except for the 1949 Weymann-bodied PD2s, their shapely lines often compromised by repanelling and rubber glazing-strip. From 1961 to 1966 garage renovations were carried out at Macclesfield, Glossop and Matlock, Charles Street workshop also being dealt with, in 1964, and finally a new combined bus station and garage in Oldham opened in 1966, all of which must have improved staff morale.

The end of the Bristol era (or so it seemed) came with the withdrawal of the last L5G saloons in 1964 and the indestructible prewar K5Gs in July 1965. An obscure casualty was a facility hitherto enjoyed by an impecunious hill-farmer who lived by the 109 route from Matlock to Ashbourne and augmented his meagre pension by breeding animals. Having habitually been allowed to stow a couple of hog-tied calves in the boot of the L5G/Weymann that had long served the route, he was inconsolable when drivers would not let him load them through the rear emergency door of newly allocated 44-seaters!

The AEC Renowns were not particularly handsome vehicles, although their 75-seat Park Royal bodies had more style about them than some of their kind. On a local service, No 979 of 1963 sits out a steady downpour in Northwich bus station in May 1965. *Author*

Renown 964 has just pulled onto the New Mills, Hayfield and Bramhall stand by the Plaza steps at the rear of Mersey Square to work a short journey on the New Mills route to Marple; by the mid-1960s this had more logically been renumbered 28x, ex 27x, reflecting the fact that it followed the route of the 28 (Hayfield) service rather than that of the 27 along the A6 towards Buxton. *Photobus*

Contemporary with the Renowns were the first Alexander-bodied Daimler Fleetlines, which started a new series of fleet numbers. Here No 1 of 1963 picks up in Chadderton on route 2 from Newhey to Manchester's Stevenson Square, a service operated jointly with Oldham and Manchester Corporations and the northern part of a short-lived cross-city 'limited-stop' service initiated in the late 1920s by the latter's General Manager, Henry Mattinson. *Photobus*

Subsequent batches of Fleetlines were given larger route-number displays. With a Crosville FS-type Bristol Lodekka (DFG65) in the background, a newly commissioned 182 displays this feature as it leaves Crewe bus station on 17 August 1965. A system of forced-air ventilation on these buses meant the loss of almost all direct cooling for passengers. *Ken Swallow*

A half-and-half dual-purpose livery applied to some later Tiger Cubs and Reliances in the 1966-8 period, together with conversion to one-man-operation, led to their gaining 'A' suffixes to their fleet numbers. No 795A of 1960 is seen at one of the eastern extremities of the company's core operating area at this time, Sheffield's Pond Street bus station. *Photobus*

End of an era. The postwar Bristols with Weymann and Willowbrook bodies were the last L5G saloons in service, surviving until 1964, and although No 99 of 1946 was a slightly early withdrawal it deserves illustration for uniquely having had its indicator box reduced in height, perhaps as a 'Dunham experiment'.
Ian Allan Library

Delivered in December 1950 as the very last new L5G, Weymann-bodied 309 runs into Flash village on a Saturdays-only offshoot of the Buxton–Leek service on 26 October 1963, only weeks before withdrawal.
A. Moyes

A carefully composed view of a Stockport Leyland PD2A/Crossley at Chorlton in September 1964 turned into a panic shot as North Western K5G No 438 sped past, definitely at the end of its life, having hit a low bridge, and on its way to dealer Frank Cowley, judging from the Salford trade-plate.
Author

85

The company's engineers again exercised initiative when faced with replacing the last half-cab saloons on the indirect 98 service from Altrincham to Warrington. Underfloor-engined buses were too high to negotiate the tight arch under the Bridgewater Canal near Dunham Woodhouses, and even some postwar half-cab saloons had been barred from it. The solution in 1964 was the acquisition of 10 of the innovative Bedford VAL twin-steer chassis with small-diameter wheels, on which were mounted 52-seat Strachans bodies with arc-shaped roofs. They suited the purpose admirably, although their lightweight construction led eventually to structural failure, prompting withdrawal when their initial seven-year CoFs expired. Replacements would arrive in 1971 in the shape of Bristol REs with 49-seat ECW bodywork, exceptionally having a similar roof contour.

There was also a move to expand the still-profitable express-service and private-hire sectors, by again buying vehicles built as luxury coaches. This resulted in the ordering of successive batches of Leyland Leopards with coachwork by Plaxton (1963 and 1971), Harrington (1964/5) and Duple (1964/6-8). Leopard/Alexander Y types fitted out as coaches continued to appear almost every year until 1971, primarily for the London services, which were becoming much more popular as the scope for motorway running steadily expanded. The unusual suffix letters by then displayed (*e.g.* 'X5L', 'X5Z') were those allocated by Midland Red to the route variations and helped to avoid confusion in seat-charting, for which that company was responsible

for passengers from Birmingham, whether southbound or northbound. London Coastal Coaches did the charting north from London to Birmingham, and North Western south from Manchester to Birmingham, and the respective charting offices were responsible for any duplication needed over their sectors. The renewed emphasis on express services raised traffic by 5% in the financial year to March 1966 alone, aided by new services to Aberystwyth, Barmouth, Pwllheli, Whitby, Cleethorpes and, soon afterwards, even to Lowestoft (again), Ramsgate, Folkestone, Eastbourne and East Midlands Airport, amounting to 70 such services overall, not counting two for visitors to distant HM prisons and about two dozen more operated solely during local 'Wakes Week' holidays.

The last great policy change in fleet replacement came in August 1967, when North Western was more than willing to be the first BET company once again to order Bristol chassis, a mere two years after the demise of the earlier generation. The opportunity arose after Leyland had acquired (from the Transport Holding Co, at Government instigation) a 25% share in Bristol Commercial Vehicles and ECW, thereby allowing sales to non-THC fleets. This 40-strong batch of short RESL chassis with Gardner 6HLW engines and 45-seat Marshall bus bodies to BET design did not arrive until early 1968, ironically just as North Western became a THC subsidiary, following BET's sale of its British bus interests to the State sector.

Two of the 1963 Duple-bodied Bedord SB3s are seen at Charles Street in 1967 after gaining NWRCC colours and fleet numbers 991/4. They ran in the main fleet for just one season, after service in blue and cream for Altrincham Coachways and Melba Motors. Between them stands 1957 Tiger Cub 702, bereft of much decorative trim and newly repatriated from Melba for one final summer. *F. P. Roberts*

▲ One of the SB5/Duples bought for Altrincham Coachways in 1964 was 987, seen that July at Aberystwyth in company with Harrington-bodied AEC Reliances of Western Welsh and Yelloway of Rochdale. It would be sold after three seasons. *Author*

▲ North Western's return to a policy of buying full-specification coaches resulted in the acquisition in 1963 of a pair of Leyland Leopards bodied by Plaxton, which builder's products had not previously featured in the fleet. This view of 963 on service from Manchester was recorded at Gloucester Green, Oxford. From 1972 to 1975 this coach would serve as Crosville CLL919. *Photobus*

The company had a second Harrington phase with the commissioning of a trio of bodies on Leyland Leopard chassis, delivered in 1965. For the following season only they were repainted for operation by Melba Motors, which nicely dates this photograph, apparently taken in the parking area at Blackpool's Coliseum coach station. Alongside is a similar coach in the Trent fleet. *F. P. Roberts*

In the late 1960s Duple Northern was also favoured with modest orders for coachwork on Leyland Leopard chassis, 255 being one of a final three delivered in 1968. Working in June 1972 for the rump of the company left after dismemberment, it is seen leaving Bolton's Moor Lane bus station on a motorway variant of the renowned X60 service from Manchester. *Photobus*

Portraying the attractive three-colour dual-purpose livery, AEC Reliance/ Willowbrook 854 of 1961 takes a breather at Crosville's Edge Lane, Liverpool, garage in the mid-1960s, having worked in from Winsford and Northwich on the service acquired in 1959 from A. E. Bowyer & Son. *Adrian Such / Les Simpson collection*

A tranquil scene inside Glossop garage indicative of fleet variety in the late 1960s. Prominent is a 1960 Leyland Tiger Cub/ Willowbrook, recently equipped for one-man operation. In the background, from left to right, are a 1966 Leyland Leopard PSU4/Duple coach, a 1961 AEC Reliance/Alexander DP and a 36ft Reliance/ Willowbrook of 1963, while on the right can be seen the rear of a Park Royal-bodied AEC Renown dating from 1964. *Photobus*

▲ Seen at Matlock on 29 October 1967, 907, one of the 36ft Alexander-bodied Leopards of 1962, was still in coaching livery but would shortly be reclassified as an OMO dual-purpose vehicle, here already being used on the 4 from Buxton to Derby; it would later pass to SELNEC PTE. Its companion, a veteran Royal Tiger/Weymann of 1953, was by this time one of the last eight of its type in service and would be withdrawn just six months later. *Author*

The same year brought changes with much greater implications, as foreknowledge of the provisions of the Transport Act 1968, had probably been the catalyst for BET's divestment and the formation of the National Bus Company out of the THC. The Act was also the instrument for the creation of Passenger Transport Authorities and Executives in major conurbations. Just in time to deal with this difficult situation, Robert Brook took over the General Managership from Bill Leese, who was elevated to the corresponding post at Ribble, in the footsteps of his predecessor, George Brook. Great uncertainty was caused by the planned November 1969 inauguration of the PTE for the Manchester area — South East Lancashire, North East Cheshire (SELNEC) — for within its territory lay six of North Western's 12 garages, along with more than half the fleet and most of the profitable services (many operated jointly with constituent municipal undertakings), which propped up the loss-makers in rural districts. Protracted negotiations were held to resolve the situation, and during North Western's short remaining spell in traditional form longer Bristol RELLs, with Leyland engines and either Marshall or Alexander Y-type bodywork, entered service. In 1971 some 35 ECW-bodied REs were expected, along with 25 Bristol VRT

double-deckers, but of these only 16 RELL buses (including nine with 'Dunham' roofs) were to enter service before the year-end.

A mutually acceptable formula could not be found for North Western to continue operating as an agent for the PTE without losing control over a critical part of its operation and yet still meet NBC objectives. It was therefore decided that vehicles, premises (apart from Manchester and Wilmslow garages), staff and services within the SELNEC area should pass to the Executive and that the remainder should be split between adjoining NBC operators Crosville and Trent. To facilitate the handover to the PTE a new company, cumbersomely entitled 'North Western (SELNEC Division) Road Car Co Ltd', was registered in November 1971, owned initially by the 'real' North Western but established to transfer assets and services to the PTE at the turn of the year; by March 1972 it had been renamed as the 'SELNEC (Cheshire) Bus Co Ltd, distinguishing it from the other divisions into which the PTE was organised. In the same month the Road Car's assets at Biddulph, Macclesfield and Northwich (a Pyrrhic victory there, at last, perhaps?) were transferred to Crosville, while Trent gained its allotment at Buxton and Matlock, both transactions being backdated to 1 January.

In the heart of Derbyshire's High Peak, 272 represents the new generation of Bristols, RESL6G models with Marshall 45-seat bodies, liveried in a pleasant variation of the contemporary layout. It is on the once-daily through run of the 185 from Bakewell to Monsal Dale, with solid evidence of country-running on its side panels. *Photobus*

An interesting nearside view of RESL 297 of 1968, at the Horwich End, Whaley Bridge terminus of the sparse weekdays-only service to Chinley. This bus would pass to SELNEC in 1972. *A. Moyes*

In deceptively pleasant weather at Higher Delph, in the last year (1970) of the Huddersfield–Oldham local service, RESL 302 sports the final bus livery. Note in the background the 'Snow Warning' board, indicative of winter conditions experienced in this part of the Pennines. *Photobus*

Alexander bodied the longer 1969 Bristol RELLs as 49-seaters, and most, like 316, were fitted with a farebox for one-man operation. Pictured in Buxton, it is heading up Terrace Road towards the Market Place from the shopping centre in Spring Gardens, a severe test of a driver's skill in wintry weather, commonplace at the town's 1,000ft altitude. *Photobus*

Full circle. The replacements for the 'Dunham' Bedford VALs were ECW-bodied Bristol RELLs, albeit with a special roof profile. The first numerically was 373, seen here in Altrincham bus station on a local fill-in trip to Sinderland Estate, properly route 183 rather than 36 (by then 'Warrington') as displayed. *Howard Piltz / Ian Allan Library*

Displaying the company's latter-day bus livery, AEC Reliance 807 of 1960 stands in Northwich bus station on a local service on 9 October 1971, less than three months before the axe fell. *Author*

Thereafter the North Western Road Car Co (at the time of its division still in profit, be it noted!) — continued as an NBC subsidiary, albeit in highly attenuated form, operating 84 vehicles from its Manchester garage (off Chester Road), concentrating solely on express and private-hire activities, and still controlled Lower Mosley Street coach station through the Omnibus Stations subsidiary. However, the latter was living on borrowed time, closing down in May 1973, express services being transferred to very inadequate facilities at Chorlton Street. The Charles Street complex in Stockport had passed to SELNEC and later became the base for PTE coaching activities. Perforce, North Western's administration had to be relocated, Wilmslow briefly becoming the unlikely beneficiary, although the garage there had closed in December 1971. In September 1972, when General Manager Robert Brook transferred to Midland Red, the registered office moved again, to Ribble's headquarters in Preston, which took control of engineering and operations. Thus five Bristol RELH/ECW coaches delivered in 1972 — the last to arrive in cream and red — gained Cheshire rather than Stockport registrations, and the very last order, for five Duple-bodied Leyland Leopards, arrived early in 1974 registered in Lancashire.

By contrast the VRTs, which arrived so late as to be delivered direct to SELNEC in 1973, were based mostly at Stockport and bore that town's registration letters in the AJA-L series, serving as an echo for another 13 years or so of the true 'North Western' era!

North Western's new Preston base became the focus for NBC's policy of segregating coaching from bus operations in the region, thereby incorporating appropriate Ribble and Standerwick express services. In the autumn of 1973 the registered office moved yet again, this time to Manchester's Chorlton Street coach station, and five months later, in February 1974, the company name was formally changed to 'National Travel (North West) Ltd'. In the meantime, in 1972, the fleetname had been changed to '**NATIONAL**', with '**NORTH WESTERN**' shown (on Manchester-based vehicles) only in much smaller lettering on the forward panels; even that was to disappear by 1978, whereupon all reference to the proud North Western company disappeared — apart, perhaps, from the odd abandoned timetable case in deepest Cheshire or Derbyshire. The name was to re-surface in 1986, being revived for a new company formed to take over Ribble's Merseyside services in readiness for bus-service deregulation, but that, as they say, is another story.

Sic transit gloria mundi. Northwich garage in transition, epitomised here by 384, one of the few 'normal' Bristol RELL/ECWs to be painted in NWRCC livery, AEC Renown/Park Royal 978 of 1963, already in Crosville guise, and 1966 Daimler Fleetline/Alexander 194, displaying Crosville fleet and route numbers, on 23 April 1972. *Author*

A pair of ex-North Western Alexander-bodied Leopards, caught in Northwich bus station soon after passing to Crosville. Foremost is FJA 223D (now CLL929) still in NWRCC coach livery, with VDB 961 (CLL917) astern, repainted in the CMS equivalent. New service numbers have also been allocated. *F. P. Roberts*

Ordered by North Western but delivered direct to SELNEC PTE were 25 ECW-bodied Bristol VRTs which would have confirmed the 'Tillingisation' of the company. The indicator layout was that of the new operator, although local trade-union objections ensured that an intermediate blind was not fitted for a long time. Appropriately on the NWRCC 71 route to Altrincham via Gatley, 402 (intended as NWRCC 420) speeds past ex-Stockport PD3 No 94 at the Cheadle Old Road, Edgeley, terminus of the 330 from Ashton-under-Lyne, on 11 August 1973. *Author*

A 49-seat Alexander-bodied coach new in 1968, Leopard 266 (KJA 266F) stayed with its original owner. At a location it must have passed many times previously, it is seen emerging from Great Bridgewater Street 'tunnel' under the Central Station site, opposite Lower Mosley Street coach station in November 1973, just six months after the latter's closure. No-one would then have guessed that above this very spot within 20 years there would be an attractive bowstring-girder bridge for an LRT line (Metrolink) to Altrincham — nor that the railway station would become a major exhibition and conference venue. *Author*

The Congleton–Buxton route epitomised much of North Western's territory in Derbyshire, contrasting sharply with the profitable townscapes of Greater Manchester. This scene features preserved Bristol L5G No 270 of 1946, fitted in 1958 with a second-hand Willowbrook body dating from 1952.
R. Fielding / Greater Manchester Transport Society